# Managing the Welfare State

Under Mrs Thatcher, the Conservatives promised to change everything. Public sector management was transformed in the 1980s by the wholesale importation of private sector management techniques, in response to a new concern with efficiency and the proper allocation of resources.

As the economic miracle of the 1980s fades into memory, the resulting economic and social disaster – and the failure of public sector management – is hard to ignore. Where did the Conservatives go wrong, and what can be done?

Managing the Welfare State differs from other books on public sector management in its sharply political and intellectual approach. It is a fiercely argued root-and-branch critique of new public sector techniques, and vigorously opposes the agenda of reform which in the authors view has even been assimilated by Labour and continues to inform British social policy to the present.

**Tony Cutler,** Senior Lecturer in Sociology, Middlesex University
**Barbara Waine,** Principal Lecturer in Social Policy, Middlesex University.

# Managing the Welfare State
## The Politics of Public Sector Management

Tony Cutler
Barbara Waine

**BERG**
*Oxford/Providence*

First published in 1994 by

**Berg Publishers Limited**

Editorial offices:
221 Waterman Street, Providence, RI 02906, USA
150 Cowley Road, Oxford, OX4 1JJ. UK

© Tony Cutler and Barbara Waine 1994

**Library of Congress Cataloging-in-Publication Data**

**British Library Cataloguing in Publication Data**

ISBN 0 85496 843 1 (cloth)
1 85973 011 6 (paper)

Printed in the the United Kingdom by Short Run Press, Exeter.

# Contents

# List of Tables

# List of Abbreviations

| | |
|---|---|
| A and E | Accident and Emergency |
| AES | Alternative Economic Strategy |
| CCT | Compulsory Competitive Tendering |
| CIP | Cost Improvement Programme |
| CT | Competitive Tendering |
| CVCP | Committee of Vice Chancellors and Principals |
| DES | Department of Education and Science |
| DHA | District Health Authority |
| DHSS | Department of Health and Social Security |
| DLO | Direct Labour Organisation |
| D of H | Department of Health |
| DSO | Direct Service Organisation |
| EC | European Community |
| EMS | European Monetary System |
| ERM | Exchange Rate Mechanism |
| FMI | Financial Management Initiative |
| FPC | Family Practitioner Committee |
| FTE | Full-time Equivalent |
| GPFH | General Practitioner Fund Holder |
| HMI | Her Majesty's Inspector |
| LACSAB | Local Authority Conditions of Service Advisory Board |
| LEA | Local Education Authority |
| LMS | Local Management of Schools |
| NAB | National Advisory Body (for Local Authority Higher Education) |
| NHS | National Health Service |
| PCFC | Polytechnics and Colleges Funding Council |
| PI | Performance Indicator |
| PRP | Performance-related Pay |
| RAWP | Resource Allocation Working Party |
| RHA | Regional Health Authority |
| SSD | Social Services Department |
| UFC | University Funding Council |
| UGC | University Grants Committee |
| WTE | Whole Time Equivalent |

# Preface

A crucial characteristic of discussions of social policy in the 1980s and 1990s has been the salience of management issues. In the National Health Service (NHS), in personal social services and in higher education a central area of debate is the expected effects of the introduction of 'quasi-' or 'internal' markets: both prior to, and parallel with, this development changes in the organisation of public sector services meant that, increasingly, units providing services have been given a degree of financial autonomy. Under Local Management of Schools (LMS) school governors have been given discretion to manage school budgets; the NHS and Community Care Act 1990 created 'Self-Governing Trusts' which meant that units such as hospitals, previously controlled by District Health Authorities, could apply for Trust status and would henceforth derive their income from selling their services; university departments have become cost centres; and local Direct Service Organisations (DSOs), providing services such as refuse collection, are obliged to keep separate trading accounts and meet financial targets set by central government.

Such changes have also been reflected in the language used in the public sector and in conceptions of the occupational identity of staff. Techniques associated with the private sector, such as the use of business planning or management accounting, have been introduced into the public sector (Basford and Downie 1991). New instititutions, congruent with these developments, have also been created. The National Audit Office and the Audit Commission were established. These bodies act as agencies monitoring the practice of central goverment departments and local authorities (and the NHS) respectively and, via 'value for money' reports, attempt to promote what they see as good management practice.

In general and, with respect to specific techniques, a concern with management in the public sector was not a novel phenomenon in British politics: The idea of introducing private sector management concepts was embodied in reports such as that of Fulton (1968) on the civil service. Equally, contracting out of services, such as cleaning and catering, occurred in central government departments and the NHS in the 50s and 60s. This was, by no means a preserve of Conservative governments, the initiative in introducing contracting out of cleaning in central government departments came from Labour in 1968 (Ascher 1987: 24–5). The Layfield Committee (1976), on the financing of local government, suggested the establishment of a body similar to the Audit Commission (McSweeney 1988:30).

However, what was different about the 1980s was the systematic introduction of managerialism, a processs which drove the plethora of institutional changes referred to above. In a general sense, public sector managerialism is characterised by the belief that the objectives of social services such as health, education, personal social services or social security can be promoted at a lower cost when the appropriate management techniques are applied (see Pollitt 1990a: 2). This book is concerned with both the general link between managerialism and politics and with four distinct manifestations of managerialism. These four aspects are: (1) the emphasis on the measurement of 'performance' and the use of performance indicators, which is examined in chapter 2; (2) the character of quasi-markets and the issues raised by their introduction in chapter 3; (3) the use of compulsory competitive tendering (CCT) in local authorities and in the NHS in chapter 4; and (4) pay determination in the public sector, which is analysed in chapter 5. Chapter 1 and the Conclusion (chapter 6) set public sector manageralism in the context of political developments. The book is centrally concerned with British politics and the public services in Britain, but throughout, these changes are set in the context of broader trends, in particular in the United States and the European Community (EC). The Conclusion looks at the future of managerialism in the light of the Conservative Party's fourth successive term in office following the 1992 general election. However, to understand the emergence of contemporary managerialism, it is essential to consider the changes wrought during the 1980s, and these are analysed in chapter 1.

# 1

# The Politics of Manageralism

In this first chapter the aim is both to characterise contemporary managerialism as it has impinged on the social services in a general sense and to situate this phenomenon politically. The latter objective is particularly crucial and is central to the whole thesis of this book. A striking feature of managerialism has been that the key initiatives have not, in general, emanated from public sector bodies providing services, such as schools, universities or social service departments, from intermediary bodies like Regional or District Health Authorities or from local government. Rather, these initiatives have come from central government: Local Management of Schools (LMS) was introduced in the Education Reform Act 1988, which also gave the polytechnics 'corporate status', rendering them independent of local authorities, and created a quasi-market in this sector of higher education (subsequently, the division between universities and polytechnics has effectively been removed). The development of sets of performance indicators has mainly come at the instigation of central government (a topic developed in chapter 2), and in areas such as health and housing their content has been directly determined by the central government departments involved. Compulsory Competitive Tendering (CCT) in the NHS was introduced by the then DHSS in 1983, and in local government by the Local Government Act 1988.

It is this very dominance of central government with respect to changes in the management of public sector services which raises the key question: How does managerialism relate to the politics of the Conservative administrations since 1979 and to the ideological framework within which policies were justified, and, to some extent, formulated? It is this question that this chapter begins to address. Begins, because the Conclusion will examine policy since the change of Conservative leadership from Margaret Thatcher to John Major. The chapter is divided into three sections: the first develops a more detailed characterisation of the central elements of public sector managerialism;

1

the second looks at the ideological shifts in Conservative politics, in particular the emergence of 'New Right' doctrines; and the third considers the relationship of Conservative political practice to New Right ideology, and seeks to locate managerialism with respect to this relationship. This discussion of the relationship between politics and managerialism is designed to underpin the specific critical analyses of particular features of managerialism in chapters 2–5 and to provide a basis for the analysis of developments in the 1990s in chapter 6.

## Contemporary Public Sector Managerialism

There are, necessarily, difficulties in attempting to characterise the managerialist approach to public sector services in the British case when the phenomenon is diverse and the sources are varied. The argument, therefore, takes as its focus two central reports: the Griffiths Report (1983) on general management in the NHS, officially entitled 'NHS Management Inquiry', and the Jarrett Report (1985) on management structures in the universities.

Both reports exemplify the pattern already identified, namely, the initiating role of central government. In the case of Griffiths, Norman Fowler, the Secretary of State for Health and Social Security announced in February 1983 that he had asked 'four leading businessmen' to prepare a report on the 'effective use of manpower and related resources in the National Health Service'. The time-scale envisaged for the completion of the report was a short one and the report was brief, appearing in the form of a 24-page memorandum to the Secretary of State dated 6 October 1983, and subsequently published on the 25th of that month (Harrison 1988: 60). In contrast, the Jarratt Report was not commissioned by central government but by the Committee of Vice Chancellors and Principals (CVCP). However, Sir Keith Joseph, then Secretary of State for Education, made it clear, in a speech in the House of Commons on 28 March 1984, that central government had not played a passive role in this. He stated, 'in request to my wish that there should be an efficiency study in the universities the Committee of Vice Chancellors and Principals have proposed, *and I have agreed*, that the study should be conducted under their aegis' (Hansard 1983–4, Col. 205, Vol 57, Parliamentary Debates; our emphasis).

In both cases the reports had an influence on policy in their respective fields. This was particularly the case with Griffiths, where the major recommendations were accepted by government (Harrison 1988: 62). Central here was the proposal to appoint general managers at Regional and District Health Authority and Unit levels. In the case of Jarratt, the impact was less marked. Some of its recommendations such as the need to develop performance indicators, were taken up by the CVCP (Cave 1991: ch.1). In addition, a policy of selective allocation of research funding, favoured in the report, was adopted but this reflected an established bias to selectivity which already pervaded government policy (Cutler 1992a: 2–3). However, what is significant is the intellectual approach informing these documents, and what it tells us about contemporary managerialism.

In both cases the reports draw their preferred form of organisational structure from the private sector. That is, a multi-divisional organisation, where a relatively small head office at the apex of the corporation interacts with a series of operating divisions (for the similarity of this model with Jarratt, see Williams and Williams 1987). The head office role is to formulate strategy, that is, decide which businesses the corporation should be in, whether growth should be pursued via organic development of existing businesses or via acquisitions, and to allocate capital between divisions. Head office also monitors the divisions by scrutinising their financial status. Such monitoring would, in turn, influence capital investment and decisions on whether particular businesses or divisions would be retained or divested. Consequently, while units are accorded a degree of *operational* autonomy, they are subject ultimately to control from the top.

In the Griffiths Report this distinction is made in the recommendations for the role of different levels of the organisation. Thus, Griffiths proposed that a Health Services Supervisory Board be established whose role would be the 'determination of purpose, objectives and direction for the Health Service; approval of the overall budget and resource allocations; strategic decisions and receiving reports on performance and other evaluations from within the Health Service' (Griffiths 1983: 3). The NHS Management Board was to operate at the next level down, and its main role would be to 'plan implementation of policies' but also monitor performance (ibid.).

The monitoring of operational performance thus called for general management at lower levels of the structure since responsibility for operational performance had to be located:

> one of our most immediate observations from a business background is the lack of a clearly-defined general management function throughout the NHS. By general management we mean the responsibility drawn together in one person, at different levels of the organisation, for planning, implementation and control of performance. (Griffiths 1983: 11)

A similar idea operates in Jarratt. On the role of Vice Chancellors Jarratt argued: 'The tradition of Vice-Chancellors being scholars first and acting as a chairman of the Senate and carrying out its will, rather than leading it strongly, is changing. The shift to the style of chief executive, bearing the responsibility for leadership and effective management of the institution is emerging and is likely to be all the more necessary for the future' (CVCP 1985: 26). As in Griffiths, if universities were to be accountable operational units, they would need general managers.

A correlative feature of this approach was the need for a flow of information (mainly upwards) on performance. Here Griffiths and Jarratt claimed that both the availability and use of data on performance was inadequate. On the NHS: 'it still lacks any real continuous evaluation of its performance...rarely are precise management objectives set; there is little measurement of health output; clinical evaluation of particular practices is by no means common and economic evaluation of those practices extremely rare' (Griffiths 1983: 10). While Jarratt argued: 'far more work needs to be done on measures of output' and that data was 'currently used for administration and not for management' (CVCP 1985: 19).

Information on 'performance' was also, as in the multi-divisional organisation, to influence resource distribution. This emphasis was much more marked in Jarratt: 'in most cases resource allocation does not appear to take into account the relative strengths and weaknesses of departments' (CVCP 1985: 18). The Report went on to mention, with approval, two universities where a percentage of non-salary funds had been allocated in proportion to research income raised by the department; however, this was an exception rather than the norm (ibid.).

The resource allocation pattern in health at the time of the Griffiths Report, was designed to distribute resources according to a measure of 'need', determined by a formula devised by the Resource Allocation Working Party (RAWP) in 1976 (for a description of the formula, see Mays 1987: 47–8). Given this framework, there were obvious constraints on a policy of selective rewards and punishments in accordance with measures of performance. However, Griffiths did argue that, 'cost improvement programmes can and should be initiated within the NHS ...these should carry with them the incentive that a significant proportion of the savings made can be used *locally* to bring about further change and improvement' (Griffiths 1983: 13; our emphasis).

Griffiths and Jarratt both found the multi-divisional form of organisation appropriate to the public services of their investigation. Yet this response raises further questions regarding the assumptions made in their arguments.

A striking feature of both Reports is their abstraction. The reader would learn much more about the views of the authors on management, organisation structure and control than on substantive issues arising from the services themselves. This is, in fact, a crucial feature of managerialism. The central issue is the form of management adopted; the activity being managed is at best a secondary matter.

Thus, whether this form of management is appropriate to the service concerned is barely addressed. Griffiths does acknowledge the issue: 'We have been told that the NHS is different from business in management terms, not least because the NHS is not concerned with the profit motive and must be judged by wider social standards which cannot be measured' (Griffiths 1983: 10).

The response to this objection is rather summary. Griffiths argues that, in the private sector, profit targets do 'not immediately impinge on large numbers of managers below board level' (ibid.). Consequently, if non-financial targets, such as attaining productivity or quality levels, are used in the private sector, what is to prevent their use in the public sector? Thus a second key assumption is that management information is relatively transparent, that is to say, it is clear what constitutes a standard of performance and that such standards can be measured relatively unproblematically. This position, as we shall discuss in more detail in chapter 2, does not address the complexity and ambiguity of measures of public sector performance.

A final key element in managerialism in public sector services is its implications for professional practice. A central feature of education, health and personal social services in particular is that important decisions involving the deployment of resources are made by professional staff. Equally, these groups do not fit easily into the multi-divisional structure because of its hierarchical character. Consequently, managerialism operates in a state of tension *vis-à-vis* professionalism. These tensions are brought out much more explicitly in Jarratt, where there is a clear anti-professional message: it is argued that, with restraints on university funding, they should be more selective in the range of activities that are pursued, but that such policies had been resisted, with attempts made to retain the existing distribution of resources between subject areas. This is explained in the following terms: 'among the reasons for this are the strong forces within each university. These include large and powerful academic departments together with individual academics who sometimes see their academic discipline as more important than the long-term benefit of the university which houses them' (CVCP 1985: 22).

The approach to this question in Griffiths is much more *sotto voce*: clinicians are merely to be involved 'more closely in the management process, consistent with clinical freedom for clinical practice' (Griffiths 1983: 6).

However, it is difficult to see how the multi-divisional structure can operate without attempting to subordinate and control professional practice. The whole approach stresses that those mobilising and utilising resources at an operational level be accountable to higher levels of the organisation. In this respect the Griffiths approach is unstable since if doctors are to be no more than *invited* to be involved in relating their workload to budgetary constraints, then, quite clearly, they can choose not to do so. Furthermore, investigations of the impact of general management in the NHS have shown that where reviews of clinical activity have taken place, they have concentrated on concerns of professional practice rather than making explicit links to the costs of clinical decisions, as in the Griffiths prescriptions (Pollitt et al. 1991: 69).

Griffiths and Jarrett thus give a guide to the key interlocking elements of contemporary managerialism, as it has been applied to public sector social services. The approach is hierarchical in the sense that at least the superordinate targets are set at the top, and monitoring, while a pervasive feature of the organisation, is ultimately controlled from the top. It is assumed that the structure is universally valid, can cut across public and private sectors, and is applicable whatever public service is considered. Since performance monitoring is crucial, it is assumed that valid management information can be developed. Finally, the hierarchical characteristics of the structure create tensions with the role of professionals in public services. Thus professional practice, in so far as it involves making decisions that commit resources and is a significant resource cost itself, should be incorporated into the management process of accountability. This in turn can take place in various ways: professionals themselves can be turned into managers. Jarratt's objective of transforming Vice Chancellors fits into such a model – professionals can be turned into budget-holders; simultaneously, attempts can be made to subordinate professionals by inserting them into a chain of command in the management hierarchy.

These elements of managerialism have clear links with a number of the developments, which will be discussed later in the book. Since management information plays a central role in this structure there is necessarily an emphasis on performance measurement. The link with 'quasi-markets' would seem to be somewhat more ambiguous. Such markets have either been introduced or are planned to operate in health, personal social services and higher education. In some respects this mechanism appears to involve less central government control. Quasi-markets require 'providers' to bid for resources by contracting with 'purchasers'. This gives the provider unit greater freedom, in the sense that it can choose a mix of activities on which it may decide to concentrate, which may differ from the historical pattern of its activities.

However, it is important not to exaggerate the extent of decentralisation implied in quasi-markets (this point will be developed in chapter 3). In all cases the quasi-market works within a context of predetermined public policy objectives. These have implications for the operation of the 'market': for example, maintaining access to services, particularly in the case of health, means that the scope of the unit to choose the activities in which it will specialise is circumscribed. Similar considerations bear on the extent to which competitive pressures will operate to determine how many provider units stay in the market. Centralisation also operates with respect to purchasers so that, for example, local authorities are required to submit their community care plans for approval to central government.

A similar hybrid combination involving elements of market mechanisms and central control operates in the case of CCT (see chapter 4). The compulsory element here extends not just to the obligation to tender for the services covered, but also to a complex regulatory framework, which seeks to determine the criteria used in the evaluation of tenders. Similarly, implicit in many variants of managerialism is the adoption of incentives linked to 'performance'. This, in turn, has influenced attempts to change the pattern of public sector pay determination by the introduction of performance-related pay (PRP) and pressures to decentralise pay determination, an issue discussed in chapter 5.

Public sector managerialism is thus directly linked to a hierarchical approach in which central government has operated as a prime mover. This means that, if we are to understand this development, it is essential to relate it to the political ideology and practice of the party which was continuously in office during the 1980s: the Conservative Party.

## Ideological Shift: the Impact of the 'New Right'

In this section we shall examine the implications of a major ideological shift in the Conservative Party, which dates from the mid-1970s. This phenomenon is often characterised as the rise to prominence of a doctrine referred to as the 'New Right'. Before discussing this in detail, however, it is worth making the point that the influence of the New Right in general, and on conservative parties worldwide, has been varied. It has been most pronounced in Britain and the United States, particularly under the governments headed by Margaret Thatcher and Ronald Reagan. In contrast, in areas such as labour market deregulation (see p. 19 below) and privatisation, the impact on continental European EC members has been much more circumscribed.

To understand the distinctive character of the New Right it is necessary to set it in the context of the ideological stance that dominated British Conservative politics in the period from the end of the Second World War to the mid-1970s. A good example of this approach comes in the published writings of Harold Macmillan, Conservative Prime Minister from 1957 to 1963, and previously Foreign Secretary and Chancellor of the Exchequer. Throughout his political career Macmillan had supported a form of capitalist economy with substantial state intervention both to regulate the economy and to ensure minimum standards of social provision. In the 1920s he had advocated the development of employment protection legislation to extend individual rights (e.g. through limits on working hours) and to impose obligations on employers to engage in collective bargaining (Eccleshall 1990: 180). Later he became an enthusiastic advocate of Keynesian economic policies, and his overall political stance has strong affinities with a 'liberal collectivist' outlook, combining state intervention to ensure minimum standards with a capitalist economy free to operate with respect to provision above the minimum (Cutler et al. 1986: 27 and 41).

The ideological tenor of Macmillan's position can be captured from his most representative work, *The Middle Way* (1938). In this book he argued: 'For as far ahead as we can see, it is both possible and desirable to find a solution of our economic difficulties in a mixed system which combines State ownership, regulation or control of certain aspects of economic activity with the drive and initiative of private enterprise...' (cited in Eccleshall 1990: 193). He went on to describe his ideal social and economic form of organisation as 'planned capitalism, or as it may be, a new synthesis of Capitalist and Socialist theory' (ibid.). Such a social order he saw as a precondition for preserving...civic, democratic and cultural freedom' (ibid.).

During the inter-war period Macmillan was an oppositional figure on the left of the Conservative Party. However, the concept of the 'middle way' swiftly became an orthodoxy in the post-war period (Eccleshall 1990: 184–7). It was this position, as much as explicitly socialist arguments, which New Right thinkers took as the focus of their criticism.

*The Hayekian Critique:Political Philosophy*

The extent of New Right work poses problems of selection. However, because his work covers issues of both political philosophy and political economy, the argument here takes the work of Friedrich von Hayek as a reference point. During the 1980s an interesting feature of the way in which right-wing policies were presented is that they often drew on a political language formerly used by the political left. Thus, Conservative policies have often been described as 'radical'; Thatcher and Reagan were said to have effected 'revolutions', and, of course there is the 'New' Right. This tends to obscure the fact that such positions are often a re-presentation of well-worn positions. This is true, not just with respect to the nineteenth-century lineage of New Right thinking, but also of Hayek's own career. Thus, one of his most famous attacks on economic planning, *The Road to Serfdom*, was published in 1944 and he continued working for the next thirty years as a relatively marginal figure both intellectually and politically until his views gained increasing currency in the 1970s and 1980s.

The first major difference between Hayek's approach and the liberal collectivism of the 'middle way' is his conception of the proper role for the state. Macmillan's view of the role of the state in ensuring proper economic regulation and minimum social standards involved a capitalist market economy, but one with a substantial sector of nationalised industries operating as state monopolies, extensive employment protection legislation and a welfare state with a virtual state monopoly supply of services, such as health and education. Hayek was consistently and trenchantly opposed to all these: his general commitment to competitive markets led him to oppose any state monopolies of economic activity (Hayek 1960: 224). Although not against the state provision of a minimum income, he argued for compulsory social insurance so that, as far as possible, individuals should not 'become a charge on the public'(ibid: 280). Equally, the role of the state in social insurance would rule out monopoly state provision; the state would mainly operate in social insurance on an analogy with car insurance, making individual insurance obligatory, but leaving provision to predominantly private (or voluntary) suppliers (ibid.: 292). This approach led Hayek to attack health care systems like the NHS where provision free at the point of use is combined with tax finance (ibid.: 298). Finally, Hayek consistently repudiated Keynesian economic policy (see p. 12 for further discussion).

Central to Hayek's argument for a highly restricted role for the state in social and economic policy is the 'anti-rationalist' aspect of his political thought. In particular, he argues that planning, whether social or economic, assumes an ability consciously and rationally to understand and manipulate social and economic mechanisms. However, this involves a basic misunderstanding of the nature of social order: 'the case for individual freedom rests chiefly on the recognition of the inevitable ignorance of all of us concerning a great many of the factors on which the achievement of our ends and welfare depends' (Hayek 1960: 29).

It is such ignorance that underpins the value of reliance on market mechanisms. Markets work by the mutual adjustment of individuals to signals, and this unconscious and unplanned mechanism ensures that 'more knowledge is utilised than any one individual possesses or than it is possible to synthesise intellectually' (ibid.: 30). It is interesting to note how far this Hayekian language and form of argument had, by the mid-1970s, been assimilated by prominent British Conservative politicians. Thus, in his *Stranded on the Middle Ground*, the title itself redolent of a repudiation of the Macmillan approach, Sir Keith Joseph argued: 'the market system is the greatest generator of national wealth known to mankind: coordinating and fulfilling the diverse needs of countless individuals in a way which no human mind or minds could ever comprehend, without coercion, without direction, without bureaucratic interference' (cited in Eccleshall 1990: 238).

In line with Hayek's advocacy of a restricted role for the state was his criticism of another central feature of social democratic thought and its accommodation by Conservative politicians of the Macmillan persuasion: the pursuit of social justice. This goal has often been seen as at least part of the rationale for universal welfare services, and certainly for a system of progressive direct taxation where higher rates of tax are paid at higher income levels. It has already been pointed out that Hayek was a critic of a comprehensive state welfare system. He was also opposed to redistributive social and economic policies and progressive taxation, favouring proportional rates which would be invariant with increased income (Hayek 1960: ch. 20).

Hayek's attack on redistributive policies and on the concept of social justice can be approached from two distinct but related angles: what he saw as the contradiction between such objectives and the conditions of individual freedom; and what he saw as the conceptual confusions surrounding the concept itself.

For Hayek the pursuit of social justice meant that society should be organised in such a way that it becomes possible 'to assign particular shares of the product of society to different individuals or groups' (Hayek 1976: 64).

This objective is seen as a threat to freedom in two senses: Hayek argues that the state must intervene to ensure that 'particular people get particular things' (Hayek 1960: 259–60), which involves 'discrimination between and an unequal treatment of different people' (ibid.). However, not only is the pursuit of social justice discriminatory, it implies an inevitable expansion of the role of the state. Hayek argued that the attempt to combine the objective of social justice with a market economy is bound to fail. Social justice, in his view, requires an attempt to ensure that each individual obtains his or her 'just' reward. However, market economies are characterised by endless adjustments, which simultaneously change relative earnings. Market economies are thus continually operating to subvert and undercut the 'just' distribution of incomes. Consequently, the logic of the pursuit of social justice is to restrict the role of the market and move towards a command economy. Thus, he argues that social justice can 'be given a meaning only in a directed or "command" economy...in which the individuals are ordered what to do...' (Hayek 1976: 69).

This argument has important political implications. Advocates of the 'middle way', whether in conservative or social democratic parties, while anti-communist, drew a clear distinction between 'mixed economies' with a substantial welfare state and the command economies of the former Eastern bloc countries. For instance, the original edition of *The Middle Way* displayed the swastika and the hammer and sickle on the dust-jacket; the middle way was the alternative to totalitarianism. In contrast, in Hayek, social democracy and collectivist conservatism were not benign alternatives to a command economy, but carried within themselves the seeds of such a development.

The second line of Hayek's critique of the pursuit of social justice turns on what he saw as the confusions inherent in the concept. Debates on social justice have often referred to the effects of impersonal social forces magnified by the operation of market mechanisms. Thus, the various effects of unemployment or ill-health, or changes in the economic structure, create a distribution of resources unrelated to the merits of individuals. Hayek fully accepted that such processes do operate and, in fact, he was critical of authors who 'have defended free enterprise on the grounds that it regularly rewards the deserving...' (Hayek 1976: 74) He argued that it was understandable that 'people resent that their remuneration should in part depend on pure accident', but 'that is in fact what it must if the market is to adjust itself...and the individual is to be allowed to decide what to do' (ibid.: 81).

Furthermore, such processes were not pertinent to concerns of 'justice', since what is 'just' or 'unjust' concerns relations between individuals, not the effects of impersonal forces: 'Justice requires that in the "treatment" of another person or persons certain uniform rules be observed' (ibid.: 70). Consequently, it is a misuse of terms to apply justice or injustice to 'the manner in which the impersonal process of the market allocates command over goods and services to particular people'

11

(ibid.). Tomlinson (1990) neatly summarises Hayek's position that where the concept of social justice is used a *double* error is made, since the concept is inappropriately applied to the distribution of rewards, which, being unintentional, can neither be just nor unjust; and the pursuit of social justice involves genuine injustice since individuals must be treated in a discriminatory manner (Tomlinson 1990: 18).

## The Hayekian Critique: Political Economy

A central element of Hayek's defence for a highly restricted role for the state lies in a specific political philosophy. However, this argument is also articulated with a distinctive approach to political economy at whose centre was a consistent critique of Keynesian economic policy.

Keynesian 'demand management' exerted a substantial influence over political ideology and practice in the period between the end of the Second World War and the 1970s. Unemployment, it was argued, stems from a deficiency of aggregate demand and could be controlled and minimised by a variety of means at the disposal of government: increases in public spending, tax reductions, an expansionary monetary policy. This appeared to allow not just a solution to the problem of unemployment but also, by precluding the onset of depressions, promoted a higher and more consistent rate of economic growth. This in turn fuelled optimism on the viability of the 'middle way', since it allowed for both higher levels of private consumption and of public social welfare spending. As Table 1.1 shows, these objectives were attained consistently in the era of the 'long boom'.

**Table 1.1** Average annual growth rates of final consumption expenditure per head, real government consumption expenditure and rates of unemployment in the OECD countries, 1960–73

|  | 1960–68 % | 1968–73 % |
| --- | --- | --- |
| Growth of real final consumption per head | 3.7 | 4.0 |
| Growth of real government expenditure | 4.7 | 2.5 |
| Unemployment as a % of total labour force | 3.1 | 3.4 |

*Source*: OECD (1987)

It is important to stress that, while Keynes emphasised the importance of deficiency of aggregate demand as the principal cause of mass unemployment, he did not exclude other causes. Thus, both Keynes and subsequent Keynesian commentators have accepted that there are structural causes of unemployment. For instance, particular levels of regional unemployment may be inflated by that region having an unfavourable industrial structure dominated by declining industries. However, a feature of the Keynesian approach has been the argument that levels of structural employment are significantly influenced by the level of aggregate demand (Thirlwall 1981: 21). Thus, for instance, structural unemployment could be reduced in a context of higher growth in part because it would promote a higher level of vacancies in areas with a more favourable industrial structure, which will encourage labour mobility.

Hayek was a consistent and long-run critic of both Keynesian economic theory and the broad political economy that accompanied its emergence as an orthodoxy. This is hardly surprising since Keynesian demand management represents a form of 'rationalism', that a capitalist economy can be organised to achieve predictable goals. In contrast to Keynes and subsequent Keynesians, Hayek looked at unemployment as a predominantly structural problem. Thus, he argued, 'the older, and to me convincing explanation of extensive unemployment ascribes it to a discrepancy between the distribution of labour (and other factors of production) between different industries (and localities) and the distribution of demand among their products' (Hayek 1978: 200).

Hayek not only treated structural unemployment as independent of the level of aggregate demand; he took the view that Keynesian policies *exacerbated* structural distortions. For example, he inverts the Keynesian view in arguing that labour mobility is *encouraged* by lower levels of aggregate demand (Hayek 1967: 274).

Consequently, Keynesian approaches both fail to recognise the underlying causes of unemployment and reinforce rigidities and lack of adaptation in the market. The result of such policies was a mechanism for increasing inflation, since the control of unemployment would depend on policies to expand demand, which would involve spiralling inflation: 'the amount of expenditure which would have to be incurred before the demand for the kind of services which the unemployed offer may have to be of such a magnitude as to produce major inflationary effects before it substantially increases employment' (ibid.: 272).

The commitment to full employment is thus seen as involving a vicious circle, since maintaining high employment levels in the light of structural maladjustments means courting inflation, which, in turn, is an obstacle to adjustment: 'the chief harm which inflation causes...[is] that it gives the whole structure of the economy a distorted, lopsided character... . It does so by drawing more and more workers into kinds of jobs which depend on continuing or even accelerating inflation' (Hayek 1978: 192).

The Hayekian attack on Keynesian macro-economic policy articulates a vital strand of his thought and of the New Right in general: the critique of 'producer groups'. From this standpoint, a crucial obstacle to the adjustments required in, and made possible by, a market economy is the action of organisations of producers who operate to promote their 'special interests' at the expense of the public interest.

In Hayek's case the principal manifestation of the attack on producer groups is his hostility to trade unions. This follows from the assumption that the market should optimally function as a self-adjusting mechanism. Trade unions intervene in this process by altering relative wage levels and acting to limit the freedom of employers to control the means of production. As far as Hayek was concerned, these effects were wholly negative. He claimed that trade unions had depressed the overall level of real wages (Hayek 1960: 271); that they discourage investment levels because they are able to reduce significantly returns to capital (Hayek 1967: 285 and 286); and they increase inequalities in wage levels between union and non-union labour by means of the exercise of 'monopoly' power, thus creating a wage gap which has 'no foundation' in efficiency differences (Hayek 1960: 271).

Given the negative role ascribed to trade unions, the critique of Keynesian economics is thus reinforced. Not only is a commitment to full employment seen as strengthening the hand of trade unions against employers, it insulates unions from the effects of their own restrictive practices. Thus, as there is a commitment to full employment, government is required to use monetary and fiscal policy to sustain employment whatever the inefficiency of labour or the wage levels demanded (Hayek 1960: 281)

## Professionals as Producer Groups

So far in this section the discussion of the critique of producer groups has concentrated on Hayek's arguments on trade unions. This broad approach has also been taken up by other New Right authors to analyse those key players in welfare services: professional groups. The attack on the professions is similar to that on trade unions: the professions are accused of seeking to establish a monopoly over service provision; to fix job territories so that they cannot be entered by non-professionals, thus boosting professional job security, increasing costs and rendering working practices rigid.

However, whereas the power of trade unions is seen to be located in a combination of special legal privileges (see p. 17 below) and the guarantee of full employment, the power of professional groups is seen to lie in the conditions of the regulation of social services established by the state. This regulation relates both to the demand for social services and over the supply of professional labour in the provision of these services.

On the demand side, while government-supplied services like health and education in the United Kingdom have never had a strict monopoly, state provision has occupied a dominant role since the end of the Second World War. Table 1.2 shows the breakdown of the UK school population between state and private sectors.

**Table 1.2** UK Schools' Population by Sector 1961, 1971, 1981, 1990 (000s)

|                | 1961 | 1971 | 1981 | 1990 |
|----------------|------|------|------|------|
| Public sector  | 8102 | 9507 | 9866 | 8477 |
| Private sector | 680  | 621  | 619  | 613  |

*Source*: CSO (1992: Table 3.5)

Furthermore, state provision has operated by supplying a service, financed predominantly by taxation, where the character and extent of the service has been determined by government. For the New Right this operates to reinforce the power of professional producer groups by insulating them from the effects of market competition and consumer choice. Since the overall funding of the service is determined politically, consumer choice can only operate in the limited area of private practice. While the global pattern of provision is determined by funding and regulatory decisions made by government, professionals are, according to the New Right, able to determine service standards at the micro-level. Thus, for example, in the case of health care in Britain, Green argues: 'The NHS provides a standard considered acceptable by doctors within the budgets available to them' (Green 1990: 11).

A preferred New Right stance, and one consistent with Hayekian precepts, is to use a 'voucher' system. This system operates by providing a public subsidy in the form of a voucher of a given value, which can be used to purchase a given service. Under such schemes public service suppliers are obliged to compete with private or voluntary sector alternatives, and voucher holders may purchase the service where they will. Green (1988: 74) provides a recent example in proposals for reform of the NHS. He envisages vouchers for primary and hospital health care whose value would vary with the age of the individual and which could be used at either private- or voluntary-sector suppliers. Individuals under

15

this scheme could remain in a tax-financed NHS but, if the voucher option were chosen, would opt out of the NHS, although they would retain the right to free NHS long-stay care (Green 1988: 76).

New Right authors on social welfare also want to take supply-side deregulation further than total or partial privatisation of service provision. In particular, they are concerned that professionals operate what they see as unnecessary restrictive practices in defining entry qualifications and in the control of who does what job. Thus, Chubb and Moe have argued for a system of education allowing any group to set up schools and receive state funding provided they meet minimal standards of teacher certification (Chubb and Moe 1990: 219). Such schools would have complete freedom over issues such as admission requirements, and structure of government and organisational form, although they would be accountable to the state for pupil performance.

It is clear that New Right thought represents a radical break with the premises of both social and economic policy involved in post-war social democracy and the liberal collectivist conservatism of Macmillan's 'middle way'. Both these strands, in their different ways, envisaged a mixed economy with a substantial welfare state in which producers, whether trade unions or professionals, were partners. The New Right envisages a minimal state operating within a legal and regulatory framework, which constrains the power of producer groups. However, if we are to attempt to situate where public sector managerialism fits in with respect to this ideological set it is necessary to look at the relationship between the New Right and Conservative political practice.

## The Conservatives and the New Right: Tempering the Shift with Political Expediency

Reference has already been made to the extent to which Conservative politicians in the 1970s and 1980s assimilated the concepts and language of the New Right. In addition to Sir Keith Joseph's Hayekian paean to the market, he made a clear break with 'full employment' in textbook New Right terms: 'the duty imposed on itself by the State to maintain full employment was partly fulfilled by subsidising inefficiency and technological obsolescence' (cited in Eccleshall 1990: 236). Mrs Thatcher referred in a House of Commons debate in 1981 to Hayek's *Law, Liberty and Legislation* as 'absolutely supreme' (cited in Wedderburn 1989: 7). However, rhetoric and ideological adherence are not the same thing as political practice. In this section we shall demonstrate that, with respect to the New Right, Conservative policy in the 1980s followed an ambiguous course, and that it is in relation to such ambiguity that public sector managerialism must be situated.

To illustrate the character of this ambiguity three areas of policy will be considered: (1) the position of 'producer groups'; (2) the role of the state with respect to social services; and (3) the policy of privatisation.

## The Attack on the Trade Unions: the Gospel of Individualism

As we saw above, a central plank of New Right ideology is the attack on producer groups. This is one area, as Wedderburn (1989) has cogently demonstrated, where, at least as far as labour law is concerned, Hayekian prescriptions have been particularly influential.

To understand the nature of the transformation it is necessary to set the changes effected during the 1980s in the context of approaches to labour law, which had previously occupied a dominant role in twentieth-century British politics. Central to this earlier view was a linked set of assumptions: that the contract of employment was qualitatively different from other contracts; and that it involved a fundamental asymmetry in the respective powers of employer and employees. The assumption was, therefore, that *unorganised* employees had unequal bargaining power relative to employers, and that it was incumbent on the state to redress this balance. This took the form of establishing the legal conditions within which trade unions could operate and establishing a floor of statutory employment rights on wage levels, hours of work, health and safety, and so on. It is interesting to note that, even at the outset of Mrs Thatcher's first administration, this broad conception was still being advanced. In introducing the 1979 Employment Bill the then Secretary of State for Employment, James Prior, stated: 'The law should always give full recognition to the inherent weakness of the individual worker *vis à vis* his employer, to the need for him to be organised in a union and to the need for his union to have such exceptional liberties as may be necessary to redress the balance' (cited in Wedderburn 1989: 3).

The reference to 'exceptional liberties' referred to the peculiar and specific character of the treatment of trade unions in British law. Continental European jurisdictions have tended to recognise various 'positive' rights associated with trade unionism, such as the rights to organise collectively, bargain and strike (Wedderburn 1989: 4–6). As a corollary, in these jurisdictions, where industrial action is either threatened or taken, this does not involve a breach of the contract of employment. In Britain the whole issue has been treated differently. The threat to strike is usually a threat to break the contract of employment.

Consequently, unless legal protections were given trade unions and their officials would have been vulnerable to civil actions for torts such as inducing a breach of a contract of employment. The particular form which these protections have taken has been to give what has been termed 'immunities' against common law liabilities.

Thus, in a strict sense, British immunities were designed to achieve the same objective as positive rights in the continental European jurisdictions. However, the very use of this term has unfortunate connotations since it gives the impression that trade unions are given preferential treatment, a feature illustrated by Prior's reference to 'privileges'. This is a perennial theme in Hayek's arguments: 'unions have not achieved their present magnitude and power by merely achieving the right of association. They have become what they are largely in consequence of the grant, by legislation and jurisdiction,of unique privileges which no other associations or individuals enjoy' (Hayek 1967: 281).

It is, of course, important to stress that the idea of state intervention operating to achieve a 'balance' between employers and employees was susceptible to a variety of readings. On the political left, for example, collective bargaining and the related strengthening of individual employment rights was, not surprisingly, pursued more vigorously than on the right. However, these were arguments not about whether the state should intervene to offset the bargaining weaknesses of the individual employee, but rather what the appropriate measures to strengthen the hand of labour should be.

To the New Right it is clear that such a concept is anathema. It involves directly intervening in the market by means of restrictions on conditions of employment and strengthening a key institution, the trade unions, which act collectively to limit the control of employers over the production process. Equally, it implicitly assumes the goal of social justice by refusing to accept the verdict of the market as a given.

As Wedderburn (1989) demonstrates, the 1980s saw a Conservative government embracing the Hayekian message in a series of legislative interventions with respect to both collective and individual labour law.

In the field of collective labour law what is striking is the pronounced individualist bias embodied in the legislation. For example, since 1984 trade unions have been required to undertake a ballot of their members before taking industrial action. The Employment Act 1988 states that a union is prohibited from expelling or penalising a member because the latter has worked in defiance of a *majority* decision to strike in a ballot (Wedderburn 1989: 24). This condition applies even though the dissident member is in breach of his or her obligations under contract in union rules (ibid.). In other words, the legislation embodies a marked hostility to collectivism, even if the latter is underpinned by democratic decision-making and contractual relations.

A similar example is provided by the treatment of so-called 'secondary' industrial action. For example, in 1980 solidarity action and picketing away from the worker's place of work was prohibited. In 1982, this prohibition was extended to action to help workers obtain recognition for bargaining purposes or even consultation (Wedderburn 1989: 27). Wedderburn calls this 'enterprise confinement' an attempt to limit industrial action so that collective solidarity across firms and sectors is eliminated (ibid.).

Parallel developments have occurred in individual labour law. The Conservatives adopted a deregulationist labour approach to the labour market. This meant that a whole series of protections with respect to pay and conditions were removed. An example which gives the flavour of this ideological and political shift and its reflection in policy is the approach to unilateral arbitration. Under this mechanism it was possible to extend the terms of voluntary collective agreements to employers who had not been party to them (Wedderburn 1986: 344–5). This policy could operate when the collective agreement was established by an employers' organisation and workers representing the workforce in the employments concerned. Such legislation embodies a whole series of collectivist assumptions including: that it is legitimate to override individual contracts, since the terms and conditions set by arbitration were incorporated into the contracts of employment if the original contract terms were less favourable than the 'recognised terms'; and a *de facto* encouragement to the recognition of trade unions. Not surprisingly, such measures were set aside in the 1980s labour market deregulation programme. Unilateral arbitration was abolished in 1980 (Wedderburn 1989: 17). It is also worth noting that while measures of labour market deregulation were introduced in a number of EC member countries in the 1980s, in Britain this was far more extreme. Here the pattern has been to remove the legal protections concerned. It has been much more common in other EC countries to redefine the legal protections rather than remove them altogether (Wedderburn 1989: 20–1).

Many of these measures are significant because they have strengthened the hand of employers, but they are equally significant in setting an agenda for debate. In particular, they have contributed to a climate in which New Right hostility to the interests of producers has been accepted as a given parameter, and this has been particularly true where these producers are working-class, manual workers. This theme will be developed in chapter 4.

Conservative initiatives in individual and collective labour law follow a New Right agenda. However, this is not a general phenomenon. In particular,the New Right agenda has been effectively repudiated in the social services.

### Safe in our Hands? The Absence of Privatisation in the Welfare State

This agenda does not require complete privatisation of the social services. What it does demand is that state provision should operate in a market in which the state limits its role to either minimal regulation (as in the Hayekian model of compulsory insurance) or, at least, as in voucher schemes, allows for mechanisms to opt out of state provision. In both approaches what is envisaged is competition between providers and that the overall distribution of resources in the service is, if not wholly determined, at least heavily influenced by consumer decisions.

This is *not* the programme the Conservatives have adopted with respect to the principal social services. In all cases the overall level of service financing has remained politically determined and is, in general, subject to cash limits. In health, personal social services and higher education quasi-markets have been established that involve divisions between a 'purchaser' and 'provider' role. In principle this increases the scope of competition between the providers. However, the purchasers are not service users but rather professionals or managers in government agencies or local government. Equally, as we shall demonstrate in chapter 3, such markets are controlled by very substantial regulations on the activities of purchasers and providers. The quasi-market is *par excellence* the managed market.

It is also worth bearing in mind that the compromise involved in the adoption of quasi-markets, in many respects, replicates analogous features in the programme of privatising formerly nationalised industries. From a New Right standpoint a change in the ownership of the assets concerned is in itself a secondary issue. What is crucial is that privatisation ensures that effective competition occurs. However, privatisation of utilities like British Telecom and British Gas were effectively privatisation of monopolies where the consumer interest was to be protected by the appointment of regulators working within a pre-set framework of price control. Yet such controls were rejected by Hayek as involving a slide towards further mechanisms of control over the enterprise (Hayek 1960: 222).

### Managerialism and Conservative Politics

Conservative policy in the 1980s thus involved a mixed legacy. There has been a very marked ideological shift to hostility to producer interests and this has been reflected in labour market deregulation, anti-trade union legislation and policies which have significantly contributed to the creation and perpetuation of mass unemployment. On the other hand, the New Right agenda has not been generally followed. In both social welfare policy and privatisation, policies antipathetic to the New Right have been adopted.

This raises the question, how does public sector managerialism respond to this contradictory politics? On the one hand, managerialism, as was argued earlier, is essentially consistent with the anti-producer group stance so characteristic of New Right ideology and which is a central feature of Conservative politics in the 1980s and 1990s. On the other hand, there are crucial and significant differences between the managerialist and New Right projects. The central figure in the Hayekian world is the entrepreneur, whose role is to adjust flexibly to the demands and requirement of the market. The essence of this role is its opportunistic character. For Hayek there can be no rules of entrepreneurship; the market itself is simply a 'discovery process' (Hayek 1978: ch. 12). Nothing could be further from the approach of managerialism. Reports such as Griffiths and Jarratt espouse a prescribed model of managerial practice, which embodies what are seen as appropriate structures and techniques. Similar managerialist presumptions pervade the activities of institutions such as the National Audit Office and the Audit Commission. What is assumed is a rule-governed diffusion of best practice.

The Griffiths and Jarratt prescription is thus based on a corporate capitalist conception, or at least the kind of organisational form which has prevailed in Anglo-US corporate capitalism. Yet Hayek's relation to the modern corporation is, in fact, an ambivalent one. For instance, in an essay on the 'The Corporation in a Democratic Society' he argued a marked anti-managerial case including *inter alia* the proposal that individual shareholders should be able to determine what share of net profits they wish to reinvest in the company rather than receive a dividend determined by management (Hayek 1967: 307–8).

A second area in which there are major contradictions between managerialist and New Right positions operates with respect to quasi-markets. These deeply offend many crucial New Right precepts. This is nicely illustrated in a critical attack, by Green on the quasi-market introduced into the NHS.

Green (1990) argues that the quasi-market proposals only mention consumer choice as a presentational device, an issue which will be explored in detail in chapter 3. He argues that, while competition between providers in the delivery of services has been introduced, it is restricted to what he calls a 'defence-industry procurement model', 'where a few suppliers tender to provide goods or services to a government specification (Green 1990: 7). The 'consumer sovereignty' approach, which Green favours, is abandoned in favour of 'a managed market where purchasers act as proxies for consumers and their contractual arrangements reached by purchasers determine the service provided which is constrained by a politically determined budget' (ibid.: 9).

In contrast, while the Griffiths and Jarratt Reports were written before the development of quasi-markets, their assumptions sit quite happily with such managed markets. Note, for example, how the features of determination of overall policy objectives for the managed quasi-market, which New Right commentators find so antipathetic, is already anticipated in the strategic determination of objectives by bodies such as the NHS supervisory board in Griffiths, and the treatment of the University Grants Committee (UGC) in Jarratt.

Consequently, Conservative social policy of the 1980s and 1990s has been a policy where managerialism has emerged at the expense of the ideology of the New Right. However, given the stridency of the ideological shift in British Conservatism and its manifestation in certain areas of policy, it is worth asking why this political option was taken.

At least with respect to social policy two related determinants stand out: the general electoral constraints on the Conservative Party during the 1980s, and the particular problems posed by the application of radical right policies to social policy.

It might seem, at one level, rather strange to mention electoral constraints when discussing the Conservative Party in the 1980s and 1990s. After all, the party has won the last four British general elections and achieved parliamentary majorities of in excess of 100 seats in two of those elections (1983 and 1987). However, as Table 1.3 illustrates, the Conservatives' election victories have not been achieved with a dominance in terms of share of the total vote. Consequently, they have remained vulnerable to relatively small shifts in voting patterns.

**Table 1.3** British general election results, 1945–92, percentage share of vote and seats won

|      | Conservative | | Labour | | Liberal[*] | | Other | |
|------|------|-----|------|-----|------|-----|------|-----|
|      | SV   | S   | SV   | S   | SV   | S   | SV   | S   |
| 1945 | 39.8 | 213 | 48.3 | 393 | 9.1  | 12  | 2.7  | 22  |
| 1950 | 43.5 | 299 | 46.1 | 315 | 9.1  | 9   | 1.3  | 2   |
| 1951 | 48.0 | 321 | 48.8 | 295 | 2.5  | 6   | 0.7  | 3   |
| 1955 | 49.7 | 345 | 46.4 | 277 | 2.7  | 6   | 1.1  | 2   |
| 1959 | 49.4 | 365 | 43.8 | 258 | 5.9  | 6   | 1.0  | 1   |
| 1964 | 43.4 | 304 | 44.1 | 317 | 11.2 | 9   | 1.3  | 0   |
| 1966 | 41.9 | 253 | 47.9 | 363 | 8.5  | 12  | 1.6  | 2   |

| | SV | S | SV | S | SV | S | SV | S |
|---|---|---|---|---|---|---|---|---|
| 1970 | 46.4 | 330 | 43.0 | 288 | 7.5 | 6 | 3.1 | 5 |
| 1974(February) | 37.8 | 297 | 37.1 | 301 | 19.3 | 14 | 5.8 | 23 |
| 1974 (October) | 35.8 | 277 | 39.2 | 319 | 18.3 | 13 | 6.7 | 26 |
| 1979 | 43.9 | 339 | 37.0 | 269 | 13.8 | 11 | 5.3 | 16 |
| 1983 | 42.4 | 397 | 27.6 | 209 | 25.4 | 23 | 4.6 | 21 |
| 1987 | 42.3 | 376 | 30.8 | 229 | 22.6 | 22 | 4.3 | 23 |
| 1992 | 41.9 | 336 | 34.2 | 271 | 17.9 | 20 | 6.0 | 24 |

* Alliance 1983 and 1987; Liberal Democrat 1992
SV = share of the vote
S = seats won
*Source*: Butler (1989); Guardian 14 April 1992

Indeed, much of the hybrid and ambiguous character of Conservative politics reflects attempts to reconcile ideological objectives with electoral calculations. The confused character of privatisation policy was referred to earlier (p. 20). In many respects this derived from a constellation of opportunistic concerns. Thus, it has been convincingly argued that at least one reason why utilities like British Telecom and British Gas were privatised as *monopolies* was that such an approach was the only acceptable one to the incumbent management, whose co-operation was vital if the privatisations were to be accomplished speedily (Marsh 1991: 467). In turn, the haste to accomplish privatisations was a response not so much to overarching ideological objectives (the term was not even included in the 1979 manifesto) as to the attractions of the policy as a means of raising revenue (ibid.: 460). Equally, many features of privatisation contained clear elements of electoral calculation, e.g. the element of underpricing of issues to guarantee take-up and profits to investors.

Thus, ideology was often tempered by electoral calculation. There were, of course, exceptions to this rule, the poll tax being the most notorious case, but, in the sphere of social policy, a strong element of pragmatism was present. To understand this pragmatism we shall need to examine whether social policy presented any special obstacles to a hard New Right programme. To do this, it is necessary to look at the evidence on public attitudes to social welfare during the 1980s.

## Public Opinion and the Welfare State

Since 1983, the *British Social Attitudes* surveys have collected data on attitudes to the welfare state – on issues such as levels of support for increases (or reductions) in spending on social welfare programmes and for public or private provision of social services. Notwithstanding the Conservative electoral success at the time, the 1983 survey showed that there was not 'an emerging strong majority determined to roll back the frontiers of the state' (Bosanquet 1984: 96); while the 1990 survey (the latest available at the time of writing) concluded that 'the 1980s have seen a strengthening of public endorsement of centralised tax-financed state welfare' (Taylor-Gooby 1991: 41).

One indicator of an 'anti-welfare' position would be the extent to which individuals favoured reductions in both taxation and welfare spending. The earlier survey found that 54 per cent of respondents favoured the status quo on taxes and spending on health, education and social benefits, while 32 per cent wanted to increase and 9 per cent to reduce taxes and spending on these services (Bosanquet 1984: 80). By 1990 the figures were 37 per cent, 54 per cent and 3 per cent respectively (Taylor-Gooby 1991: 25). Thus the proportion favouring increased spending had risen from around a third to just over a half.

In 1983, 42 per cent of Labour identifiers, 35 per cent of Alliance identifiers and 24 per cent of Conservative identifiers supported an increase in taxes and welfare spending (Bosanquet 1984: 81). By 1990, a clear majority of Labour and Liberal-Democrat supporters favoured this option – approximately two-thirds in each case – but so did a substantial minority of Conservatives, 42 per cent (Taylor-Gooby 1991: 28).

Support for disengagement of the state and the limit on state provision to a residual service role was also very limited. Thus, the 1990 survey repeated a question which was asked in 1983: whether the NHS should be restricted to those with low incomes, others above this income level being required to take out medical insurance – a position which was, as indicated earlier, in line with a Hayekian position. Support for such a two-tier system had fallen from 29 per cent to 22 per cent, and opposition increased from 64 per cent to 73 per cent (Taylor-Gooby 1991: 26). The surveys did find increasing dissatisfaction with the NHS and, in particular, with hospital services: those who described themselves as quite or very dissatisfied increased from 25 per cent in 1983 to 47 cent in 1990 (Bosanquet 1984: 86; Taylor-Gooby 1991: 37). However, the 1990 survey found that dissatisfaction was associated with the belief that government should increase taxes to pay for increased spending on the service; thus the problem was seen as one of inadequate resourcing (ibid.: 40).

Care is needed in interpreting such survey evidence, which *prima facie* contradicts material presented by Ralph Harris and Arthur Seldon of the Institute of Economic Affairs. They undertook five surveys between 1963 and 1987. These showed a high level of public support for private forms of provision. In the 1987 survey they found that 68 per cent of their respondents would accept an education voucher at full value which would allow them to send their children to private schools, although this figure was reduced when the value of the voucher was reduced (Harris and Seldon 1987: 41). Seventy-five per cent of respondents were prepared to accept a full-value voucher for private health insurance (ibid.: 47).

In part, such differences in results are determined by the character of the questions being asked. A criticism of the *British Social Attitudes* surveys is that they ask their respondents, for example, whether they support increased taxes to pay for additional welfare spending; they do not ask whether the individual respondent is prepared to increase his or her tax burden. However, similarly, the questions used by Harris and Seldon are hardly uncontentious. They ask whether respondents would accept vouchers for health care and education. This is not the same thing as asking them if vouchers would provide an acceptable alternative to state provision of services.

While it is not possible to take a definitive view on this issue, it can be argued that the evidence suggests that there were considerable political risks in attempting to pursue a New Right line on social welfare, in particular as the trends in favour of increased welfare spending appeared to be strengthening over the decade. This also had implications for another issue: public spending.

## Public Spending: Parsimony not Disengagement

The logic of New Right arguments tends to favour consumerist forms of provision like vouchers rather than direct state provision, even when it operates in a quasi-market form. Of course, in such situations, state *finance* of the service continues to operate. However, another important dimension of the New Right is the argument for state disengagement from both finance and provision of welfare except in a residual form, as illustrated in the Hayekian argument for compulsory insurance with a minimum income, discussed earlier (p. 9). The abandonment of such a New Right project had implications for public spending. If the state continued to finance and provide the major social services, then the scope for radical reductions in public spending was not present. Again, this led to New Right disenchantment with the Conservatives; writing from this position Burton published a critique of the first Thatcher administration entitled *Why No Cuts* (Burton 1984). The absence of radical change in the level of public spending on services is shown in Table 1.4.

**Table 1.4** UK general government expenditure on services in real terms, 1979/80 to 1990/1 (Expenditure in £billion, rounded to the nearest decimal point, 1990/1 prices)

| 79/80 | 80/1 | 81/2 | 82/3 | 83/4 | 84/5 | 85/6 | 86/7 | 87/8 | 88/9 | 89/90 | 90/1 |
|-------|------|------|------|------|------|------|------|------|------|-------|------|
| 168 | 169 | 173 | 181 | 183 | 187 | 187 | 191 | 191 | 187 | 194 | 195 |

*Source*: Treasury (1992b)

The figures given in Table 1.4 refer to expenditure on services. Total spending also includes debt interest, various adjustments and, in addition,the government chose to present privatisation proceeds as a negative item in striking a general government spending figure. It is worth noting another ambiguity in this respect: some commentators have viewed the privatisation process as *alternative* to deep cuts in public spending (for discussion of this point, see Marsh 1991: 462). Certainly, proceeds were very considerable in some years, for example the 1988–9 figure for this item, in 1990–1 prices, was £8.2 billion. What is certainly clear is that there was no major revolution in public spending, while there were reductions in real terms in some years, over the period as a whole, spending on services increased by just over 16 per cent.

On the other hand, the period has been experienced as one of parsimony, and in many respects this is a realistic view. For example, in a letter to the *Financial Times* Wells (11 February 1989) pointed out that, adjusting for inflation, NHS current expenditure on goods and services under the Thatcher governments from 1979 to 1988 grew at the slowest rate (1.6 per cent per annum) of any previous administration since 1954 (by contrast, the growth rate under the Heath government 1970–4 was 4.8 per cent per annum).

It is within this constellation of forces that one must situate public sector managerialism. The rejection of the New Right programme on social welfare meant that the state retained responsibility for running social services and thus had to face the expenditure implications of this option. This called for control of public spending which fitted in with the ideological and the political objectives of the Conservatives. On the other hand, control was a negative option, and managerialism offered a positive message: goals could be attained with the use of fewer resources if only the appropiate management approach were adopted. To assess how far the promise of managerialism has been realised it is necessary to look at the substantive areas of policy where managerialism has had an impact. They make up the subject of the next four chapters.

# 2

# Managing by Numbers: the Bogus Prospectus of Performance Indicators

Attempts to measure the performance of public-sector service providers are, in no sense, a new phenomenon. In a famous article, published in 1901, Sidney Webb called for an 'honorary competition' between local authorities, which would involve 'an annual investigation of municipal efficiency, working out their statistical marks for excellence' in such areas as 'drainage, water supply, cleansing...housing, hospital accommodation, sickness experience and mortality and publicly classifying them all according to the results of the examination' (Webb 1901: 378). The King was to present a 'shield of honour' to the authority which had made most progress with respect to these indicators and civic dignitaries were to be recognised by awards, such as a knighthood for the mayor of the winning council. More recently, the Guillebaud Committee, which reported in 1956 on the cost of the NHS, published a 'performance league table' comparing health authorities in terms of indicators such as length of patient stay and bed turnover (Klein 1982: 389). However, such proposals or ventures into performance measurement were isolated and had no real impact on the management of public sector services. In contrast, in the 1980s performance measures became ubiquitous: by 1985 the Public Expenditure White Paper included 500 such indicators; by 1988 this figure had increased to 2, 000 (Carter 1991: 86).

The same trend is evident in the growth of performance measures in specific services: for example, a set of 145 indicators covering the NHS was developed by the then Department of Health and Social Security in 1983 (Roberts 1990: 92); in 1986 the University Grants Committee (UGC) and the Committee of Vice Chancellors and Principals (CVCP) issued a set of 'performance indicators and management statistics' for higher education: the scope of performance measurement has continued to grow in the 1990s; the Citizen's Charter requires schools to publish their public examination results (Prime Minister's Office 1991: 14);

under the same initiative, a recent consultative document outlined proposals for indicators on personal social services to the elderly and children (Audit Commission 1992); and a Department of Environment circular of 1990 details indicators relating to housing services which local authorities will be expected to publish (Cole and Welsh 1991: 13).

## Extending Accountability

Performance measurement and review has often been justified on the grounds that it is vital to accountability. Such arguments have seen the process of electoral accountability as limited and partial. A good example is the case of the Audit Commission. This body was established under the Local Government Finance Act 1982 and came into operation in 1983. Performance measurement has been central to its work in two senses: it is required to appoint District Auditors, whose role is to satisfy themselves that 'the organisation has made proper arrangements for securing economy, efficiency and effectiveness in the use of resources.' This was an extension of the role of the auditor, which had previously been limited to monitoring the reliability of accounts and checking the legality of transactions (McSweeney 1988: 29). Thus, the extended audit role involves judgements on performance in service provision where the methods used by auditors are to follow a standard format set by the Commission (ibid.). The second key feature of the Commission's role in performance measurement is the publication of reports designed to promote 'value for money', reports which frequently include comparisons of the 'performance' of local authority service providers.

An early publication of the Commission defended such activities in terms of the extension of 'accountability':

> Councillors are...politically accountable, but interest in local elections is often quite low...accountability means more than that the accounts should be presented fairly and that councillors should present themselves periodically for election. There is a need for local authorities to check and to demonstrate that they are effective, efficient and economic. Auditors have a responsibility to satisfy themselves that the authorities they audit can do this. (Audit Commission 1983: 3)

Put in this way the virtues of performance measurement appear self-evident. After all, if the democratic process has involved checking that controls are exerted over 'inputs' (that money is being spent for the purposes intended by Parliament), why should review not be applied to the products of such public service activities? The object of this chapter is to examine such claims. The chapter is divided into four sections: the first deals with issues of definition and examines the range of variants of performance indicators and measures; the second looks at the political context in which performance measurement developed in the United Kingdom; the third considers some of the methodological and conceptual problems posed by the use of performance indicators; and the final section is an overall critical evaluation of how far performance measurement might advance accountability.

## The Concept of Performance Indicator

Central to performance measurement in the public sector has been the development of performance indicators (PIs); thus any critical discussion of performance measurement involves an analysis of such indicators. What are the distinctive characteristics of performance indicators? One way to generate a working definition is to look at the two terms 'performance' and 'indicator' and explore their ramifications. The term 'performance' implies a reference to the product of the organisation being assessed. This means that performance is not measured by looking at activities or expenditure on resources. Some indicator sets include measures, which thus cannot be regarded as relating to performance. An example would be cost data such as library expenditure per full-time equivalent (FTE) member of academic staff and central administrative expenditure per FTE student. In this case the measure is one of the use of resources not of what is done with these resources to generate a product or output (Cave et al. 1991: 22).

The notion of an 'indicator' implies a norm, as Cuenin puts it: 'when an indicator shows a difference in one direction this means that the situation is better whereas if it shows a difference in the opposite direction, then this means that the situation is less favourable' (cited in Cave et al.1991: 21). Consequently, a 'performance indicator' should have sufficient scope to cover the product of the organisation whose activities are being assessed, and should allow normative conclusions on its performance.

### Indicators and Users

Performance indicators involve deploying data to allow normative judgements of the 'product' of public sector service providers. However, this general definition must be supplemented by examining the plurality of variant forms which performance indicators may take. It was argued above (p. 28) that one of the potential attractions of PIs was their apparent role in rendering public service providers more 'accountable'. However, the notion of accountability presupposes a user of the indicators. In fact, there are a number of possible users, a feature that has implications for how performance measurement operates.

*Top-Down Accountability*

Indicators can be used by government or by government agencies. For instance, in 1986 the UGC and in 1989 its successor, the University Funding Council (UFC), undertook an exercise to rank the research activities of UK universities. This exercise had direct implications for the universities since it was used as the basis for selectively distributing 14 per cent of the UGC grant in 1986. This was scheduled to rise to 15.9 per cent in 1991/2 (B. Williams 1991: 13). Universities with 'better' research rankings thus obtained more research funding.

It would be reasonable to regard both the UGC and UFC in these cases as government agencies since, while they were free to devise the *criteria* used in determining the rankings, the *goal* of selectively distributing resources was official government policy which was consistently reiterated on a number of occassions (see, for example, Department of Education and Science 1985: 5). Not only was this an assessment of 'performance' by a government agency, it was also one that claimed to use normative standards of performance. Table 2.1 gives the five categories used to rank research in 1989 and the meaning attributed to them by the UFC.

**Table 2.1** University Funding Council research selectivity exercise, 1989: normative meaning attributed to scale points in the ranking

| Rating Point | Interpretation |
| --- | --- |
| 5 | Research quality of international excellence in some areas and of national excellence in virtually all others |
| 4 | Research quality of national level in virtually all areas |
| 3 | Research quality of national level in the majority of areas or, international in some |
| 2 | Research quality of national level in up to half of the areas |
| 1 | Research quality of national level in none or virtually none of the areas |

*Source*: Adapted from University Funding Council (1989: Annex 3)

A parallel use of PIs is where indicators are used by one level of management to judge the activities of another. This practice operated in the NHS during the 1980s through the use of PIs by Regional Health Authorities to review the practices of District Health Authorities. Thus, a study by Allen et al. (1987) looked at the use of PIs in three districts of the same Regional Authority. They found that such features as low throughput (patients treated in a given period), high or low staff levels and costs were examples of the features singled out for 'improvement' (Allen et al. 1987: 75). In a similar vein North-East Thames Health Authority used a *single* aggregate PI based on patient activity, staffing and financial results to influence targets for cost savings expected from the Districts within the Region (Flynn 1990: 191). It is worth noting here that the norms used were derived from the *current practice* of the Districts concerned and thus a deviation from the norm was a deviation from current general practice. The significance of this aspect will be discussed later.

PIs used in this way are distinguished by their 'top-down' character. What is central is that the criteria by which performance is assessed and the judgements themselves are set by a higher level of management or by a government agency with a monitoring/regulatory role. The institution being assessed may be able to make representations concerning criteria or raise questions regarding assessments of performance: the 1989 UFC research ranking exercise did extend the range of publications considered in response to criticisms by universities of the previous UGC exercise (UFC 1989); Districts questioned assessments by Region on grounds such as the accuracy of the data used or the level of aggregation of the data in the study conducted by Allen et al. (1987: 76 and 78). However, in all these cases the final word rests with the 'top'. Thus, most academic critics of the 1986 UGC research ranking had stressed that publications should be the principal means of judging university research performance and many had attacked the use of research income as an indicator (Phillimore 1989: 262). Nevertheless, the UFC continued to use both research grants and research contracts in its criteria for judging research performance (UFC 1989: Annex 1).

*Performance Assessment as 'Self-Regulation'*

In many cases of top-down assessment judgements are made of the activities of professionals. In contrast, indicators may be determined by professionals and used in a context of 'self-regulation'. The *Confidential Enquiry on Perioperative Deaths* is an example of such a use of performance measures. The Enquiry covered deaths within 30 days of an operation in three NHS Regions (Northern, North East Thames, Southern Western). It found variations in the extent of 'avoidable deaths' between surgical specialists, anaesthetists, hospitals and Regions. Equally, it drew normative conclusions identifying deficiencies in practice such as lapses of delegation, where trainees undertook work beyong their competence or instances where inadequate pre-operative assessment took place (Roberts 1990: 22). In this case the operation of performance assessment was lateral in that it was an intra-professional process designed to draw conclusions on 'best practice' and to diffuse such practice among professional staff.

## Performance Measurement and Service Users

PIs can also be aimed at service users. The clearest example of such practice in the United Kingdom is furnished by secondary education. In this case, the rationale advanced by the government for the requirement that public examination results be published was 'to assist parents in choosing schools for their children' (Mcpherson 1992).

However, it is worth noting that indicators that may function in a top-down fashion in one country can be aimed at service users in another. In higher education the dominant pattern of indicator use in the United Kingdom has been by government, government agencies and management. Yet this is by no means a universal pattern. In the United States PIs in higher education are designed for use by potential students. This also has implications for how particular measures are interpreted. Thus a managerial user in the United Kingdom is likely to interpret a high student:staff ratio as an indicator of low unit costs (in particular as academic labour costs account for around 60 per cent of total institution costs in higher education) and thus as a favourable 'efficiency' measure. In contrast, the same result might be treated by potential students as *unfavourable* since it is seen as indicative of a poor resource endowment for the college concerned (Cave 1991: 60).

## What Should be Measured?

If there are various potential users of PIs, equally there are variations in what is measured in PI sets. In particular, a good deal of discussion has centred on the broad dimensions of performance covered by what have come to be known as the 'three E's': economy, efficiency and effectiveness. In an introductory work on performance measurement in local government, the Audit Commission gives the following definitions of these terms:

*economy*...means ensuring that the assets of the authority, and the services purchased, are procured and maintained at the lowest possible cost consistent with a specified quality and quantity. *Efficiency* means providing a specified volume and quality of services with the lowest level of resources capable of meeting that specification. *Effectiveness* means providing the right services to enable the local authority to implement its policies and objectives. (Audit Commission 1983: 8)

## *The Politics of Performance Indicators*

The use of PIs is thus potentially diverse both in terms of the range of possible users and the dimensions of 'performance' which are encompassed. However, this diversity has not been reflected in the United Kingdom in the 1980s and 1990s. On the contrary, the dominant model adopted has been one where initiation, design and use have derived from government and/or government agencies. This does not mean the initiatives have flowed exclusively from the top. For example, some local authorities developed their own performance assessment schemes (Pollitt 1986: 157). Furthermore, it should not be assumed that the project met with favour only among Conservative politicians; the potential for control can appeal to senior public service officials (ibid.: 157). However, whether in specific services or with respect to the creation of monitoring bodies like the Audit Commission or the National Audit Office (with a parallel function for central government departments), the main changes have emanated from the centre.

This raises the issue of how performance measurement should be situated politically. An obvious point of reference would appear to be the link with a decline in economic performance in the advanced capitalist countries in the period since the end of the 'long boom'. However, such accounts are inadequate in that, while poor economic performance certainly exerts pressure to restrain public spending, this engenders the imperative to exert budgetary controls, not necessarily to measure and review 'performance'. This point is reinforced by the fact that the Callaghan government espoused, and practised, rigorous expenditure control without performance measurement, while attempts to control spending have operated in tandem with performance measurement under the Thatcher and Major governments (Pollitt 1986: 159–60).

The added ingredient is the significance of managerialism (ibid.: 159). Conservative politics have embraced the New Right only to a limited extent. In a context of only marginal initiatives in the privatisation of social services, they had to be 'managed'. Equally, the model implicit in Griffiths and Jarratt presupposes information on performance as a means of ensuring accountability up the managerial chain, ultimately to central government. A similar role for performance measures can be seen in management developments in government such as the Financial Management Initiative (FMI). Thus, a review of the FMI published in 1984 argued: 'More measures of achievement are needed to translate objectives for improved management into targets for individual managers who can then be held accountable for achieving an agreed level of performance' (cited in Pollitt 1986: 156).

Performance measurement is, therefore, linked with multi-divisional-style managerialism. It also has a number of politically congenial implications. Thus, an agenda of pure spending control is negative, while the emphasis on performance 'exudes an aroma of action, dynamism, purposeful effort' (ibid.: 160).

Equally, the use of PIs allows the possibility of comparisons between organisations providing services such as local government, hospitals and universities. Such comparisons permit the compilation of 'league tables' of physical measures (e.g. staff:student ratios, average lengths of patient stay) or financial measures (e.g. cost per graduate, cost per in-patient hospital case). Thus, it can be argued that, if the 'lagging' providers could match the 'best practice', then an expansion of service provision could be achieved within the existing level of resource allocation. Equally, there is a strong emphasis in PI sets on 'throughput' measures. Examples of such measures are number of students graduating from universities or polytechnics, cases treated in NHS units in a given period, and so on. In turn, such measures can be related to 'inputs' (e.g. graduates per FTE lecturer). Such PIs encourage throughput and thus stimulate at least the appearance of 'efficiency' gains, i.e. that an increased level of service provision is being made with an unchanged volume of resources.

## Performance Indicators: Conceptual and Methodological Issues

The development and use of PIs has generated considerable debate and a substantial critical literature, the latter pointing to a series of problems, both conceptual and operational.

A central issue concerns the difficulties involved in the measurement of *outputs* and the *outcomes* of public sector services. The distinction between output and outcome is significant in a number of contexts in the PI debate. Outputs are sometimes also termed 'throughputs' of the service and are measured by the flow through of service users. Thus, for example, outputs/throughputs would be quantified by the number of patients treated (in aggregate or in a particular category); pupils or students completing a course of study; numbers obtaining a degree; numbers of children placed for adoption. In contrast, outcomes refer to the *objectives* of the service *per se*. In the case of health care such an objective would be to improve life expectancy and/or improve quality of life by, for example, improving mobility, reducing or eliminating pain, increasing the range of activities which the person can perform and thus increase personal independence. Equally, a report from Her Majesty's Inspectorate indicated the following objectives of local authority spending on education to 'provide for the main ingredients of the curriculum appropriate to the various stages of education...[to] accommodate for differences in age, ability, aptitude and goal...[to] improve and update the existing and...accomodate the new in curriculum or qualification' (cited in Jesson et al. 1985: 360).

Part of the measurement problem arises from the disjuncture between output and outcome. The difficulty is easy to see: at least in principle, there is no problem in measuring output/thoughput. However, outcomes are, of their nature, much more intangible. How do we measure whether 'quality of life' has been improved? If knowledge has been developed, how do we determine whether we are adjusting to the goals of school pupils and discover whether our curriculum is appropriate?

The intangible character of outcomes means that measures are always dependent on constructs, which attempt to generate proxies or substitutes for the outcome. The central difficulty, therefore, lies in the fact that the proxy can be criticised for failing to capture the character of the outcome. A classic instance is provided by higher education. Here it has been argued that a means of measuring the impact of research is via the use of citations. The technique operates by looking at the number of times a piece of work is cited in a range of academic publications. The outcome that the citation is aiming to measure is that part of the goal of research is to contribute to the development of knowledge in a given subject area. However, the outcome is necessarily qualitative and the use of citations as a proxy is vulnerable to the criticism that it is 'a register of fashion and agreed wisdom; not necessarily of excellence' (Minogue 1986: 398–9).

It is also worth bearing in mind that, while this problem arises in a pointed form in the case of outcomes, it is not in fact irrelevant even to some output measures. For example, one dimension of research output in higher education is publications. However, aside from any qualitative issues, there is the immediate question that publications come in a variety of forms: books, articles, communications, reviews, reports; pamphlets/occasional papers. A weighting system consequently must be devised, but there is no obvious reason why one weighting system is superior to another. A study of the publications of political science academics illustrates the point. The weighting system used *inter alia* gave 10 points for a published book and 2 for articles in a 'leading journal'. Yet this raises the question why 'a book [should] be worth five times an article rather than four times or six' (Minogue 1986: 398).

One of the ways of attempting to avoid arbitrary weights is to incorporate 'expert' judgements into performance reviews. This, naturally, has a somewhat paradoxical effect. As we saw in chapter 1, performance measurement relates to managerial forms, which were concerned not just to render managers accountable but also to place professionals within the hierarchy of control. To this extent, it incorporates the ideological trend of treating professionals as suspect 'producer groups'. However, the incorporation of professional judgement into the review process means not a judgement on professional practice *per se* but a peer review in a hierarchical framework.

In turn, this option leaves the assessment open to a different form of arbitrariness, the reliance on reputational assumptions and professional biases which impart a circularity to the whole exercise. For example, clinical reviews of the appropriateness of medical practice have found systematic variations which reflect pre-existing standards. Thus a study, published in 1989, recorded the judgements of UK and American clinicians on the appropriateness of coronary angiography and coronary artery bypass (CABG) operations. The UK panel applied more stringent standards than the US. However, in turn, these judgements reflected the pattern of *existing medical practice* since, for example, CABG operations are performed roughly five times as often in the United States compared to the United Kingdom (Roberts 1990: 37).

There are similar problems of circularity and reputationalism in rankings of educational institutions. The 1989 UFC university research ranking exercise did not involve the expert sub-committees reading all of the submissions from universities, and the composition of the sub-committees involved a statistical over-representation of academics from universities, which also received high rankings (UFC 1989: 8 and 11; Cutler 1992a).

## The Question of 'Efficiency'

The fact that there are formidable problems with 'outcome' measures has a number of important effects on performance measurement. Quite clearly, it renders the measurement of 'effectiveness' highly problematic. Measures of effectiveness involve attempting to assess how far the goals of services have been attained, but such goals require reference to the outcomes of the services concerned.

Equally, there are difficulties with the concept of 'efficiency'. As we saw, measures of efficiency relate inputs to outputs, the latter usually defined in throughput terms. Seen in this way improvements in 'efficiency' are exemplified by increasing the number of pupils/students completing courses per Full-time Equivalent (FTE) teacher; increasing the number of patients treated per FTE medical staff employee and so on. In the case of the measures referred to above, agreement that an 'efficiency' gain has been achieved depends on the premise that the 'products' concerned are comparable at two points in time. A strict claim for an 'efficiency' improvement will thus mean that the same (or an improved) 'product' is produced with a smaller input of resources. If more students are obtaining degrees which reflect similar 'educational' outcomes to those that operated in the past, or more elderly people are attending a day centre which offers the same contribution to meeting 'needs', then this condition is satisfied.

Yet, if outcomes are notoriously difficult to measure, how is it possible to demonstrate that such comparability operates? In the case of education, for example, it is true that examination results can be compared over time. However, such measures are problematic as 'outcome' proxies for two reasons: they involve a simplistic reductionism whereby the educational experience can be encompassed in examination results. (Note, for example, that the HMI report cited earlier does not mention examination performance which would not be an appropriate measure of any of the key objectives which it specified; leaving this aside there is no guarantee that examination results are assessed by reference to a constant set of criteria.) Yet, if this is not the case, then results can never be compared on a constant standard over time.

These problems have links to a phenomenon which is often the subject of comment in the literature on PIs, namely, the incentive for those subject to indicators to 'cheat' by meeting goals prescribed in the indicators with no improvement or even a detriment in the service. The incentives derive from the fact that PIs are usually imposed from above and have implications for the institutions as a whole and/or specific institutional interests. These can operate directly by affecting the distribution of grant, indirectly via the effect on the demand on the service provider (a school with 'poor' examination results may attract fewer pupils, a feature which, under LMS, would reduce the school budget); or may affect specific groups such as managers on performance-related pay, where elements of the definition of 'performance' relate to PIs. In all such cases there is a clear incentive to maximise apparent 'performance' defined in terms of the indicators concerned.

This can take the form of concentrating activity on the aspects of performance that are measured: in schools, for example, making concerted efforts to improve test and examination results, possibly through coaching. It can also mean that attempts are made to manipulate performance measures: it has become increasingly common to find commentators advocating the use of 'value added' measures in assessing the performance of educational institutions. In brief this means assessing the attainment of the pupil/student on entry to the institution and comparing this with a measure when the student leaves. The difference constitutes the 'value added' and is seen, at least in some accounts, as the contribution of the institution to improving attainment. It will be necessary to return to some of the difficulties of this later, but it is easy to see that if 'value added' were included in a PI set, it would generate incentives to 'cheat', with corresponding difficulties in controlling such cheating. The 'value added' will be boosted the better the student/pupil attainment. Consequently, there will be an incentive for the institution to inflate attainment levels and the opportunity will be available in institutions (as in higher and further education) where examinations are marked internally and merely moderated externally. Such incentives could be curbed if genuinely consistent criteria could be used and enforced from year to year, but, as has already been demonstrated, this is not the case.

Analogous practices can be found in health care and personal social services: in the former targets are set for reducing average length of patient stay or increasing numbers of patients treated. In such cases managers can adopt strategies, such as discharging and re-admitting patients, which improve 'performance' on both measures, or attempt to manipulate the mix of cases treated by the unit so that relatively simple cases involving shorter stays are admitted. In personal social services it has been suggested that indicator sets should include measures such as the percentage of a given group (e.g. elderly people) who have been refused access to a service or who are on a waiting list for a service. However, as with all measures of this kind there is scope for manipulation. Thus a cumbersome process for application for a given service might reduce applications and thus cut the numbers refused the service or on waiting lists. A weakness in service provision could thus be disguised as a strength (London Region SSRG 1989).

## Ensuring Comparability

It is of the nature of performance measurement that it involves comparisons between institutions. Yet, if such comparisons are to be valid measures of 'performance', they must compare like with like. Such conditions are crucial since, if conditions of comparability are violated, then conclusions drawn from the comparison will be invalid.

Problems of comparability arise not just with respect to the output aspect, but also with respect to inputs. PIs purporting to measure efficiency involve comparing inputs and outputs; thus a more efficient service provider is one generating the same or more output from a lower input or more output from a given input. In some cases the inputs may be measured in physical terms (e.g. FTE staff measures) or they may be financial (cost per graduate in a given subject, or per patient in a given clinical speciality). Thus, for example, an issue that has received considerable attention is the nature of the relationship between expenditure per pupil in secondary education and output measures such as examination results.

Such comparisons raise issues about the composition of the school body. These have implications for how the output figures are interpreted. For example, as results will be affected by such factors as previous levels of attainment or the socio-economic status of families, adjustments to 'raw' scores are needed to obtain a reasonable comparison (see Mcpherson 1992 for an example). A school in an area characterised by social deprivation, with pupils of a relatively low level of attainment on entry, could not be expected to obtain the same level of output as a more favoured school.

When comparisons of this type are made, it is assumed that the management whose performance is being assessed is able to control expenditure patterns in the unit being managed. However, this may be a false assumption. Thus, for example, the composition of the school population also has a marked effect on the *expenditure* side. This is a function of the fact that central government requires that LEAs make specific provision for particular groups (e.g. immigrants; those with special educational needs). Meeting these conditions triggers LEA expenditure which is 'involuntary' (Jesson et al. 1985: 362). These kinds of consideration are pertinent since indicators relating output to expenditure aim to measure the efficiency of institutions such as LEAs. In such a case relating total *expenditure* to output would be inappropriate since significant elements are outside the control of the institution itself.

Comparability problems also arise with respect to the relative complexity of the task presented to the service provider. Reference has already been made to the socio-economic background of pupils and how this may affect their educational performance. Similar issues arise both in health care and personal social services. Thus, figures for hospital mortality rates vary considerably across the United Kingdom with the highest general surgery rate 4.02 per cent (Mersey) as against the lowest 2.39 per cent (Oxford). However, no conclusions can be drawn from such figures in terms of the effectiveness of hospital treatment because the results may be affected by disease severity, comorbidity (the combination of various conditions) or local policies on care for the terminally ill (a policy encouraging discharge to the home or a hospice would reduce the hospital mortality rate) (Roberts 1990: 19). In personal social services a considerable amount of work has been undertaken on the relative costs of provision across sectors, in particular comparing public and voluntary sector providers. Early work using crude cost data concluded that voluntary sector providers operated at significantly lower unit costs. However, such conclusions have been criticised on the grounds that they use 'bald' expenditure figures which fail to take into account variations in the nature of the services provided or the groups served. For example, a study of day centres for the elderly attempted to standardise cost comparisons for 'dependency' characteristics of users and the activities of units. It found that, after such standardisation cost variations were much smaller than those based on crude cost figures; and that cost differences between voluntary and public sectors varied with size, with large voluntary organisations having higher unit costs than comparable public sector units (Knapp and Missiakoulis 1982).

*The Issue of Causality*

Many of the issues already discussed with respect to comparability concern problems inherent in how far the institution whose 'performance' is being judged is responsible for its outputs/outcomes. Some of the issues encountered in the public sector have private-sector parallels. Thus studies of variations in labour productivity between plants and companies make the point that realistic comparisons must adjust for levels of capacity utilisation (Nichols 1986). Thus, the closer a manufacturing plant is working to its capacity, the higher labour productivity is likely to be since labour requirements cannot simply be reduced *pro rata* with reductions in output, at least in the short run. Similar issues apply to public sector service providers, like schools. Thus, a school with a rapidly falling roll will tend to have higher unit costs than one where the school population is more stable because of the problems of adjusting to lower levels of utilisation (Flynn 1990: 106–7). Similarly, if the number of patients in a residential home is being reduced as a result of 'community care' policies, then this will have an effect on unit costs. Running the home will mean that certain fixed costs must be incurred, but they will be spread over fewer patients thus pushing up cost per patient. Equally, costs may be further inflated because the case-mix has been changed, with the home retaining patients with the highest level of dependence who find it more difficult or impossible to function in the community (Treasury 1992b: para. 5.8).

Further problems of identifying how far a public sector service provider is able to exert control over its 'product' are thrown up by the interdependence between social services. A classic example is provided by the relationship between health and personal social services. Thus, for example, there has been a consistent trend within the NHS to reduce the average length of stay of hospital patients. In England average length of stay in acute hospitals fell from 8.6 days in 1981 to 6.4 days in 1989–90 (CSO 1992: Table 7.31). This is often seen as an indicator of efficiency, on the grounds that it allows for more intensive use of the hospitals with a greater number of cases treated in a given period of time. For a number of reasons this could be a highly contentious interpretation, but it does mean that length of stay will be used as a norm. Thus, hospitals with above-average length of stay will be seen as relatively 'inefficient' and would thus be expected to move towards a pattern of shorter length of stay. However, shorter length of stay means earlier discharge and the viability of such a policy will depend on the availability of care in the community. Consequently, a policy of keeping patients in hospital for longer periods might reflect the lack of community care provision locally and/or the demographic profile of the area (e.g. a high level of elderly one-person households) (Birch and Maynard 1986: 146). Such cases also have cost implications. Higher throughput in the acute hospital sector may cut cost per case by reducing the time spent in hospital. However, this also means that the acute unit has displaced costs of care onto personal social services and/or informal carers, almost always women.

These examples illustrate some of the difficulties in attributing blame – or for that matter praise – to institutions in public services. It is also worth noting how government policy itself generates tensions. Thus public sector services have been encouraged to maximise throughput and to reduce unit costs. However, the vast majority of services are now cash limited so that increases in throughput run up against the ceiling imposed by cash limits, thus depressing certain measures of 'efficiency' (Flynn 1986: 401).

### 'Facts' and Norms

Earlier in this chapter we made the point that, in many cases, the normative element in performance indicators was derived from the pattern of current practice. For example, Allen et al. (1987) showed that DHAs were interrogated concerning their practice when it involved divergence from the general pattern of District practice. Yet, this raises the question: what does the norm represent? By definition the indicator should reveal a standard of 'best practice'. However, the sheer weight of conceptual and measurement problems makes such a norm elusive. Yet, without such a norm there is no necessary reason to associate practice with what is desirable. Consequently, where norms are derived from the existing pattern, they create an incentive to *conformity* to that practice (Allen et al. 1987: 82; Birch and Maynard 1986: 147). The paradox is that innovative practice could be penalised, since by virtue of being innovative, it would diverge from existing patterns of resource use.

## The Extension of Accountability?

Earlier in this chapter we cited an Audit Commission publication, which argued that performance measurement could function to complement accountability through the electoral process. In this final section we shall consider such arguments by examining the relationship of performance measurement to accountability.

Any discussion of this issue must start by defining the form of accountability, what is accounted for and to whom. As has been demonstrated earlier in the chapter, the dominant form of accountability during the 1980s in the United Kingdom has been a managerialist one. Thus, indicator sets tend to be addressed to and used by management: in the NHS, for example, a study of the use of performance indicators showed marked variations between different groups, with 85 per cent of District general managers, 80 per cent of Health Authority chairs, 81 per cent of planners but only 25 per cent of doctors and 24 per cent of Community Health Council representatives stating that they used indicator sets (Jenkins et al. 1988: 19). Similarly, studies of indicator sets have regularly pointed to the limited representation of 'effectiveness' measures, for example, a classification of types of indicator in three sets of PIs, one used by a local authority, one designed to measure educational performance and the then DHSS set for the NHS was undertaken by Pollitt (1986: 162). In all three efficiency concerns were dominant, accounting for 61 per cent, 54 per cent and 43 per cent of indicators respectively while effectiveness measures were peripheral, accounting for 1 per cent, 12 per cent, and 5 per cent, of indicators respectively.

Yet if this is the case, then the idea that performance measurement could *extend* the scope of accountability appears rather lame. Indeed, the reverse has been argued. The marginalisation of concerns with effectiveness can be seen as a consequence of the framework within which PIs operate. For example, a discussion of the role of the Audit Commission has argued that, while measures of effectiveness *do* involve difficult technical issues, there is also a powerful political dimension: 'a greater focus on effectiveness could weaken the Commission's attempts to change local authorities. Influencing acceptance of reduced funding and a reduction in the scale of organisations also means cutting back on purpose. Identifying unfilled needs and demands would have the opposite effect' (McSweeney 1988: 42) On this reading, since PIs are developed within a framework where constraints over public spending are an *a priori* assumption, this imparts a necessary bias to which aspects of 'performance' are covered.

It could be argued that such positions do not come to terms with the fact that monitoring bodies such as the Audit Commission are not agencies of government pure and simple, since they have an independent status. This, for example, gives the Commission discretion to select the topics which it wishes to study and it is free to criticise government policy. Furthermore, both the Commission and the National Audit Office have exercised this power either by criticising government policy or by advocating policies which are at variance with the prevailing biases in government. For example, the Audit Commission recommendations on community care (discussed in detail in chapter 3) involved a transfer of budget and of planning powers to local authorities in contrast to the general trend, favoured by central government, to strip local government of its functions; the National Audit Office has also published a report on personal pensions which was critical of the impact on the finances of the National Insurance fund, of the subsidies to personal pensions provided by the government (National Audit Office 1990).

However, what is striking is how far such monitoring bodies reflect general assumptions of central government policy. The argument above has already shown how the Audit Commission supported the view that the local electoral process is of questionable legitimacy. Central government policy in the 1980s has introduced a series of centralising powers which have been justified in a similar terms. Equally, a context of constraints on public spending is implicitly regarded as legitimate by the Commission. In this respect, it has been argued that it 'seeks to encourage and facilitate recognition and acceptance of restraint and shrinkage; to focus attention on managing within that context; and to reduce attempts to ignore or resist central government funding reductions and their consequences' (McSweeney 1988: 39). The kinds of assumption to which McSweeney refers are a common feature of Audit Commission publications. Thus, in the *Competitive Council* (1988), it is argued that 'limitations on resources make it more important to be realistic. Plans for expanded service in one area will not be realised unless funds can be found by economies of improved value for money elsewhere (Audit Commission 1988: 6).

A similar argument could be used with respect to bodies such as the UGC and the UFC. Thus, the research ranking exercises referred to above (p. 30) worked within the policy assumption emanating from central government, that research funds *should* be selectively distributed between universities.

There is also an important contradiction in the accountability argument in its managerialist form. The multi-divisional form of management illustrated in the FMI, Griffiths, Jarratt and the Audit Commission presupposes the transparency of information on 'performance' in public sector organisations. This goes hand in hand with the imperative to introduce a performance-oriented 'culture' where managers (and professionals) respond to goal-setting and performance review.

However, a reference back to the conceptual and methodological difficulties (discussed above, p. 34) makes it clear that such transparency is simply not present. Genuine measures of performance might thus be said to involve certain conditions: that measures be sufficiently inclusive to show cases in which improvements in one aspect are being achieved at the expense of decline in other aspects; that it is possible clearly to designate responsibility for, or 'ownership' of, performance; that rigorous conditions of comparability apply.

The discussion has shown the difficulties all these aspects present. The difficulty with outcome measures means that the trade-off of throughput for effectiveness is hard to determine. This is particularly pointed where direct contradictions between elements of performance can operate; for instance, closing down branch libraries or advice centres might encourage throughput and cut unit costs at the remaining centres, but such policies compromise access and thus effectiveness.

Similarly, issues around causality create difficulties in attributing praise or blame for 'performance'. Such problems are exacerbated where there is scope for transferring costs either onto other budgets or outside the scope of public spending altogether by loading care burdens on friends or relatives.

In other words, there is a marked disjuncture between the conditions a 'culture' of performance requires and what performance measurement can deliver. This raises the difficulty that performance measurement can become a form of theatre where the 'measures' demonstrate adherence to 'managerialist' ideology, a feature which, as we shall see in chapter 5, is also, arguably, a characteristic of performance-related pay.

### Accountability to the Consumer?

The argument so far has looked at the scope for increasing accountability from performance measurement in its overtly managerialist form. A key element in the criticism of this form was that behind the claim of wider accountability was a narrow top-down agenda reflecting the concerns of central government and of the managers of government agencies.

Implicit in at least some of this criticism is the view that the narrow scope of indicator sets, and in particular the absence of 'effectiveness' measures, reflects patterns of use. Managers are concerned with staying within budget and with cutting unit costs. They are less concerned, in a context of limited resources, with whether service objectives are being met. Most sets are seen to fail as mechanisms of accountability not only because of the limit on the dimensions of performance considered, but also because of the *de facto* exclusion of a key participant: the consumer of the service. It is this group that is seen to be concerned with effectiveness, because they use the services.

Indeed, so salient is this argument that it can certainly be classed as one of the major criticisms of the practice of performance measurement in the United Kingdom. Consider, for example, the following extracts from some academic discussions of PI sets: a study of indicators in housing pointed out that, of seventy performance indicators in a set designed by the Audit Commission to assess the performance of local authority housing services, only half a dozen related to 'customer evaluation of service providers or activities undertaken' (Conway and Knox 1990: 257–8); an analysis of indicators in higher education argued: 'the group whose interests are most strikingly ignored by current PI systems is the consumers. If they had a say one would expect indicators of access, or teaching quality and of "employability" to be prominent' (Pollitt 1990b: 79).

Such arguments are also reflected in politics. Thus, in its manifesto for the 1992 election, Labour sought to outflank the Conservatives by adopting a consumerist approach to public services. This included proposals for a Health Service Quality Commissioner, an Education Standards Commission and a proposal to make it obligatory for local authorities to carry out annual surveys of consumer satisfaction (Labour Party 1992: 16, 18 and 20).

This raises the final question to be considered in this section. If managerialist accountability appears to offer a limited and biased agenda, can such defects be rectified by bringing in the consumer? There are reasons for arguing that this is another false road. The first problem refers back to the transparency issue. If performance indicators raise problems of opaqueness and ambiguity, then this will compromise accountability in whatever form, to management, government or 'consumers'.

In overtly managerialist forms of accountability this problem tends to be assumed away, as with the dogmatism implicit in the 'culture of performance'. Similar ploys are present in the work of commentators who seek to give a consumerist bent to performance measurement. For example, Pollitt argues, with respect to outcome measures, that '[i]t is increasingly possible to measure *some* outcomes or good proxies' (Pollitt 1990c: 172). In another publication he cites an example of such a proxy, the use of 'value added' measures, and criticises a higher education PI set for not citing this measure on the grounds that 'the absence of value-added measures seriously undercuts the validity of any attempt to use PIs as an aid to judging universities' contributions to the economy or society' (Pollitt 1990b: 72).

'Value added' measures are designed to contrast attainment levels on entry and on leaving an educational institution. Consequently, they can be used as a measure aimed at consumers, since comparative value added could be taken as an indicator of the extent to which the school, college or university has improved the attainment level of its students.

However, value added is a highly contentious measure. For instance, as far as higher education is concerned, it is questionable whether the idea has any conceptual validity at all. It can be argued that the very use of the term 'higher' presupposes a qualitative jump from the 'level' of education to which the student had previously been exposed. Yet value added assumes that attainment 'before' and 'after' can be judged on the same scale (Barnett 1988). Equally, even if one does not accept this argument, results will vary markedly with the weighting applied to final degree classes (Gallagher 1991: 25).

Thus there is a symmetry between managerialism and consumerism. In both cases there is an *a priori* commitment to performance measurement, which glosses over the real difficulties involved. Thus, while it is valid to argue that existing indicator sets lack effectiveness measures which would, in principle, be of value to consumers, the argument loses much of its force if such measures are questionable and ambiguous.

Finally, 'bringing consumers in' raises another rather different problem. Advocates of this position see it operating in a context in which PIs address a multiplicity of 'stakeholders', including politicians, managers, professionals and 'customers' (Pollitt 1990c: 174–5). Such extension of the range of indicators and the range of potential users is seen as redressing the biases in existing sets.

According to the agenda that combines consumerism with a correlative extension of the range of indicators, it will now be possible, in indicator sets, to have information on all of the 'E's' and to encompass the interests of the various 'stakeholders'. Yet even if one believes that it is possible to crack the problem of measuring effectiveness, there is a fundamental sense in which broadening make the problem of performance measurement *more* difficult. Central to this is the issue of incommensurability. Thus, crucial to performance measurement is the idea that it provides a basis for assessing institutional performance; schools, local authorities, etc. can be compared against each other. Yet the 'E's' represent distinct and incommensurable measures of 'performance': for instance, how does one compare an institution where throughput is high but goal attainment is questionable with another institution where the reverse is the case? This problem is rendered yet more intractable if the category of 'consumer' is considered. In fact, in many areas of the social services it is unclear who the 'consumer' is. Thus, in the case of health care, is the consumer the patient, the potential patient or, in the case of preventive health, the community as a whole? In the case of personal social services, is the consumer the 'client' or provider of informal care? Given such indeterminacy there is a case for a plurality of 'effectiveness' measures addressed to a plurality of 'consumers'.

The promise of performance measurement was that it could establish normative standards. PIs were thus not just there to give information but to indicate how well public sector organisations were run and to show who was running them better and who worse. Yet perhaps the ultimate paradox of this project is that indicator sets can be judged inadequate because they are insufficiently inclusive, that dimensions of performance escape them. On the other hand, the project of encompassing all dimensions and all interests threatens to degenerate into an indeterminate series of measures which literally don't add up. Either way the message seems blurred.

# 3

## Welfare Markets

In chapter 1 it was pointed out that a feature of Conservative politics since 1979 has been the relative absence of privatisation initiatives in the principal social welfare services. Notable exceptions were the sale of council houses, the introduction of personal pensions (even here, though, state finance in the form of discounts and tax expenditures was not completely absent), the introduction of student loans and the simultaneous freezing of maintenance grants in higher education.

It was also noted that Conservative reticence here reflected political caution. There was continued public support for the welfare state, and in particular the NHS. Thus the potential for full-scale privatisation of health, education and personal social services was limited. However, while it was accepted that public finance would continue to dominate in these areas, there was also a desire to counteract the supposed inefficiencies of the public sector by the introduction of competition.

The approach taken to achieve this has been the introduction of 'internal' or 'quasi-markets'. In this chapter the latter term is used, because the form of competition is not limited in all cases to suppliers within the public sector (Le Grand 1990).

Central to quasi-markets is the distinction between the role of purchaser and provider. The purchaser is, in effect, an agent of central or local government, funded from public sources, that contracts for services with provider units, e.g. hospitals, universities, residential homes for the elderly. Providers can be drawn from public, private or voluntary sectors and they compete for the contracts from purchasers. The expectation is that the beneficial effects supposedly associated with the market – greater efficiency, enhanced consumer choice, diversity of providers – will be replicated by the quasi-market.

In this chapter we shall discuss the role of quasi-markets as a framework within which certain public sector welfare services are to be financed and provided in the 1990s. The argument draws on examples from the three major services affected – health, community care and

higher education – and is divided into four sections. The first looks at
the patterns of finance and provision prior to the introduction of quasi-
markets; the second surveys the background to the introduction of such
markets in each of the services covered; the third considers the prospects
for quasi-markets attaining their objectives; and the concluding section
provides a discussion of some of the dilemmas and contradictions inherent in this hybrid mechanism. For example, the extent of funding of purchasers is set by political decisions and this is an aspect which has,
perhaps, not been sufficiently stressed in discussions of quasi-markets,
purchasers and providers operate in a context that is significantly constrained by central government policy.

# Before Quasi-Markets: Patterns of Finance and Provision

## The National Health Service

Prior to the introduction of a quasi-market in the NHS, the Secretary of
State stood at the apex of the system. Under the Department of Health
were fourteen Regional Health Authorities (RHAs), which both planned
hospital and community health services for their regions and then allocated resources to the next tier down, the District Health Authorities
(DHAs). The main task of the Districts was to provide hospital and community services in their areas. The other major part of the service was
the primary care sector, which was formally outside the regional and
district structure. This was supplied by GPs who were self-employed,
operating under contract to local Family Practitioner Committees
(FPCs); dentists and opticians also came under these committees. With
the exception of charges for prescriptions, and opticians' and dentists'
fees, all health care in the NHS was provided free at the point of use,
taxation being the main source of financing. Because of the importance
of taxation, resources were allocated by central government. Once the
overall budget was set, following the annual negotiations between the
Department of Health and the Treasury, money for hospitals and community health services was allocated to Regions, and subsequently
Districts, on the basis of the Resource Allocation Working Party formula (RAWP). The idea behind RAWP was that resources should be allocated on the basis of population served, weighted by age, sex and some
measure of social deprivation. Spending by regions and districts, but not
the FPCs, was cash limited.

*Community Care*

In contrast to health, community care – that is, the provision of services which vulnerable people need 'to live as independently as possible in their own homes, or in "homely" settings in the community' (Department of Health 1989d: para 1.1) – was characterised by a number of different providers and financial arrangements. Local authority social services departments were responsible for meeting social care needs in their areas. They could either provide residential, day and domicilary care services themselves or arrange for others, e.g. voluntary organisations, to do so, and reimburse them via grants or payment of fees. Health authorities had a community care dimension to their work, with the provision of day centres, community nurses, health visitors, as well as places in hospitals or nursing homes. Finally, the private provision of care, in particular residential care, had expanded rapidly in the 1980s; between 1981 and 1990 the number of elderly people resident in private and voluntary homes more than doubled (Central Statistical Office 1992: 142).

Public funding for community care came from a number of sources: central government grants and the rates (subsequently the community charge) in the case of local authority social service departments; funds allocated by the Department of Health to RHAs and DHAs for the health-based community care services and social security with the payment of supplementary benefit/income support to those eligible who were in private or voluntary homes. With the exception of the social security element, cash limits applied to spending on community care.

*Higher Education*

Until the changes following the passage of the Further and Higher Education Bill (England and Wales) in 1992, a so-called binary system operated in higher education. The two parts of the system were the university and polytechnic sectors. Until 1988 polytechnics were under local authority control.

Prior to the introduction of the quasi-market, funds were allocated to university and polytechnic sectors in a broadly similar way. In the polytechnic sector the National Advisory Board for Local Authority Higher Education (NAB), which was established in 1982, allocated grants to institutions via a 'unit funding' approach (Pratt and Hillier 1991: 6). This involved setting grant levels on a standard basis (with marginal adjustments) for each 'programme area', or subject group. Grant per student varied by programme area to reflect differences in the cost of teaching particular subjects: for instance, the cost of teaching natural science is higher than humanities or social sciences because of the need for equipment and technical assistance.

As far as universities were concerned the system for allocating grant for teaching was similar (B. Williams 1992: 1–2). Universities and polytechnics also obtained an income from tuition fees paid by LEAs for home students. In the period considered in this section, grant was financially of much greater significance than fees, but this balance has altered over time, with tuition fees increasing in importance in both absolute and relative terms. NAB and the UGC were thus both planning bodies allocating student places to universities and polytechnics with grant following such allocations. However, university funding also included a separate element to cover the costs of research. In November 1985 the UGC announced that part of the research grant would henceforth be allocated selectively by reference to research rankings of university 'cost centres'. (Some issues surrounding this exercise from the standpoint of performance measurement have already been discussed in chapter 2).

Until 1988 the source of funding for the two sectors was quite distinct: the polytechnics were under local authority control and were financed from a pool to which all Local Education Authorities contributed (Becher and Kogan 1992: 43); UGC funds derived from central government.

Certain common features emerge from the pattern of finance and provision of services in these three areas. Planning was at least designed to play a significant role in determination of the activities undertaken by provider units. Equally, criteria of resource allocation were also tied to planning decisions; RAWP was designed to measure health needs, allocations of grant for teaching to universities and polytechnics to reflect teaching costs (though the operation of both mechanisms was tempered by concerns of political expediency, especially influenced by budgetary constraints). Finally, competition played a relatively marginal role. Local authorities used suppliers outside the public sector to provide personal social services but the relationships were not usually contractual. Polytechnics and universities competed against each other to attract students and research grants but, broadly speaking, price competition did not play a role.

Competition was absent from the NHS.

## Enter the Quasi-Market

The political background to the introduction of internal markets was different for each service. In the case of health, the context was provided by the political debates in the winter of 1987–8 when Labour attacked the government on the grounds that the NHS was significantly underfunded. Initially, the Conservatives responded by arguing that since 1979 spending on the NHS had increased in real terms. This was to no avail: the response did not effectively deflect the criticisms. The then Prime Minister, Margaret Thatcher, changed tactics and announced the formation of a committee to review the financing of the NHS. Radical change in the NHS appeared to be on the cards, and certainly the New Right 'think tanks' had developed alternative approaches to health care provision such as vouchers for health care and markets for health care with US-style Health Maintenance Organisations competing for patients (Waine 1991: ch. 3).

However, the eventual outcome of the review, the White Paper, Working for Patients, was not influenced by the New Right. There was to be no change to the basis on which the service was financed (predominantly taxation); nor would Districts have to compete for funds, which would be allocated to them on the basis of a weighted capitation formula. However, a market in health care was to be introduced with the separation of the responsibility for the purchasing and providing of such care. In the future, DHAs would become the major purchasers, offering contracts and buying services from competing providers – their own units (Directly Managed Units), self-governing trusts or the private sector. In addition, DHAs would identify and plan for the service needs of their resident population. The purchaser/provider split was to be extended to general practice, with fund-holding GPs becoming purchasers of outpatient services and a defined range of in-patient services. Non-fund-holding GPs would refer their patients to hospitals with which Districts had negotiated contracts and a contingency fund would also be available for them to refer patients to hospitals with which Districts did not have contracts (extra-contractual referrals).

The National Health Service and Community Care Act 1990 introduced the internal market into the NHS in April 1991. By 1992, there were 152 Trusts and 3,000 GP fundholders (Conservative Party 1992: 27).

*Community Care*

The origins of the internal market in community care responded to two key determinants: (1) concern with the escalating costs of social security payments to residents of private residential homes and (2) the incoherent and unplanned nature of community care. Both were the focus of the Audit Commission's report 'Making a Reality of Community Care' (Audit Commission 1986). The report recommends local authorities being made responsible for the long-term care of people with mental and physical handicaps, receiving resources from the NHS and buying in specialised care from the NHS or the private sector, and of the establishment of a single budget for the care of elderly people and the mentally ill, with contributions from the NHS and local authorities. The budget would be under the control of a single manager, who would purchase services from public and private sectors. This idea was refined in the Griffiths Report (1988) and the White Paper 'Caring for People' (Department of Health 1989d). The primary function of social service departments was to assess individual need, design packages of care and secure their delivery, 'not simply by acting as direct providers but by developing their purchasing and contracting role to become 'enabling authorities' '(Department of Health 1989d: para. 3.13). Local authorities would also be required to produce and publish clear plans for the development of community care services and establish inspection and registration units to maintain standards. As with health there was to be one purchasing agent – the local authority – but the supply side was to be diverse, involving public, private and voluntary organisations.

Unlike the NHS, the internal market in community care was to be phased in. Inspection units and complaints procedures were established in April 1991; the production of community plans in April 1992, while the transfer of social security funding to SSDs and the new assessment and care management arrangements were introduced in 1993.

### Higher Education

In higher education the central changes in the introduction of a quasi-market came with the Education Reform Act 1988. Under this legislation polytechnics ceased to operate under local authority control and were given what was known as 'corporate status'. The legislation also abolished NAB and the UGC and replaced them with the Polytechnic and Colleges Funding Council (PCFC) and the University Funding Council (UFC) respectively. With abolition of the divide, these two councils merged to form the Higher Education Funding Council for England in April 1993. Similar bodies were to be established covering Scotland and Wales (Labour Research 1992c: 12).

These new institutions were to operate in a purchasing role. In the case of the PCFC it was decided to allocate grant to polytechnics in two ways: 'core funding' for 1990–1 was to be provided by guaranteeing 95 per cent of the allocation for the previous year, uprated for inflation; the other 5 per cent would be allocated by inviting bids for grant per student, at which rate the polytechnics and colleges of higher education would be prepared to enrol students. PCFC used programme advisory groups to advise it on the bids concerned. Once the allocation had been determined, it represented a 'contract' between PCFC and the institution, which would thus be expected to enrol the agreed number of students (Pratt and Hillier 1991: 14).

Institutions would be free to recruit students in addition to those stipulated in the contract. However, in the case of these students, the institution would only receive tuition fees; no funding from PCFC would be forthcoming.

A similar system was introduced in the universities except that it took a more open-ended form. The UFC set guide prices per FTE student and invited bids. In both cases the assumption was that bids would, in general, be at prices *below* guide prices. In the case of the first UFC exercise this proved a failure with only 7 per cent of total bids below the guide price, and these bids were only marginally below. However, in the case of PCFC the outcome of the first round was a 5 per cent reduction in the mean cost per student in real terms (Pratt and Hillier 1991: 78).

Undoubtedly an important element in the emergence of the quasi-market in higher education was the emphasis on increasing the participation rate in higher education within a context of budgetary constraints. This was crucial to the abolition of NAB and its replacement by PCFC. NAB proposals for the 1987 planning round suggested that, given the resources allocated by government, student numbers would have to *fall* by 10,000. This encouraged the government to respond to the promptings of the Committee of Polytechnic Directors to move polytechnics out of local authority control (Becher and Kogan 1992: 44). This ideological shift emphasising the significance of institutional 'independence' encouraged the move to a quasi-market.

In the university sector an important determinant was the policy of selective allocation of research funding. This opened up the possibility not just of separating the activities of research and teaching but also that such a differentation could be reflected in institutions, with some universities undertaking research and some functioning as 'teaching' institutions (B. Williams 1992: Appendix 2). This differentiation was congruent with a quasi-market since (within the limits of regulation) it allows universities and polytechnics that fail to attract research funds to bid lower, with the object of increasing their student numbers.

## Quasi-Markets: Achieving the Objectives?

This section evaluates the extent to which quasi-markets can be expected to realise the claimed virtues of competitive markets –

greater efficiency, consumer choice and the stimulation of a diversity of providers.

## *Efficiency: an elusive concept*

Arguments for the use of quasi-markets often cite the claim that they will improve efficiency in the services covered. However, as was pointed out in chapter 2, there are problems besetting any attempt to define efficiency in health, social care or higher education. Efficiency is defined as an input-output relation, but in public sector services outputs are diverse. For example, in the case of health, there could be improvements in life expectancy or a reduction in the effects or the elimination of various illnesses which are not directly life-threatening. These are different types of output which cannot be summed into a combined index of performance. Outputs in relation to social care are even more problematic, while similar problems apply in higher education. Not only are teaching and research diverse activities, but research itself can be viewed and assessed according to a variety of different and incommensurable criteria. Thus the research activity of a university science department could be looked at in terms of output, quality of output (as judged by peers), impact on the field or the extent to which it has practical application (Phillimore 1989: 263).

Even if satisfactory composite measures of output could be developed, it would be necessary in any efficiency measurement to assume that changes in the output derive from the effects of the input. This is difficult to demonstrate. For example, with respect to health, Parkin (1989) reports evidence from an OECD study that international differences in infant mortality rates are negatively related to per capita health expenditure. Naturally, this could be an effect of the health-care expenditure but might also reflect the fact that international comparisons show that higher health care expenditure is associated with higher per capita income, and thus richer countries (with higher per capita health expenditure) have general advantages, such as better housing, environmental protection and nutrition, and that these factors account for the link concerned (Parkin 1989: 77). Again, there are parallels in higher education. Value added measures would claim to show the extent to which an educational institution has improved the attainment of individuals who have attended it but, in addition to difficulties with the measure, there are considerable problems in interpreting *why* any improvement has occurred. Thus, it cannot be assumed that the activities of service providers are necessarily significant, since peer pressures among students could also play a role (Mcpherson 1992).

If there are major difficulties in defining efficiency in health, social care and higher education, then the reforms cannot be justified by reference to the *demonstrable inefficiencies* of these services. Certainly in respect to health, Enthoven (1985), whose ideas played such a strategic role in the whole programme, made no such claim. His arguments centred on the lack of what he regarded as *incentives* to efficiency, not agreed measures of the existing inefficiency of the service.

Consequently, the case for quasi-markets is one that is based on a set of *a priori* assumptions, which favour a general model of competition rather than identifiable weaknesses in existing provision.

It is difficult to assess such general claims for the virtues of competition, although as we shall see (p. 65) below, quasi-markets have distinct characteristics, which differentiate them from both private sector markets and theoretical models of competition. However, when matters of efficiency are at issue, it is important to consider the costs of establishing and operating quasi-markets. In a market situation the activities of the producer must be costed, purchasers billed and advertising and marketing used to increase market share (Hudson 1992: 133). These costs are commonplace in non-welfare products, but they also have a significant impact on welfare services when they are subject to competition. In the United States, for example, the move towards a more competitive structure for health care was accompanied by intensive marketing and advertising. It has been estimated that hospitals spent $1.4 billion to this end in the United States (Robinson 1990: 21). In Minneapolis, regarded as one of the most competitive local markets in health, expenditure by Health Maintenance Organisations on radio, television and direct mail advertising increased by 50 per cent to $15 million between 1984 and 1985 (Quam 1989: 116).

The quasi-markets in the United Kingdom are, of course, still in their infancy, but there is already some evidence of significant administrative and transaction costs. Additional sums of around £380 million have been provided to the NHS for 1991–2 and 1992–3 to finance the changes associated with the reforms (Treasury 1992b: para. 3.43). In higher education a study of the first round of bidding under PCFC found general agreement among senior polytechnic management that the process had absorbed a considerable amount of management time: one Deputy Director reported that preparation of the bid had involved a 'heavy' time commitment for two months and half of working time, for another 4 to 6 weeks. It also meant a backlog of work was being dealt with 6 months after the completion of the bidding process (Pratt and Hillier 1991: 54–5).

The moves to a degree of institutional autonomy associated with quasi-markets can also have an impact on a crucial input: labour costs.

This could be particularly significant in health. Until the creation of the quasi-market, the NHS has effectively been a monopsony employer, i.e. it was virtually the sole purchaser of medical labour. Thus it has been able to impose central control over the wage bill, a feature that is particularly important where labour costs account for over 70 per cent of total costs. The development of competitive providers will end this situation. Trusts will have the freedom to set their own rates of pay for all staff, with the exception of junior doctors. Evidence from the United States indicates that hospital wage rates tend to increase in competitive labour markets (Robinson 1990: 34). Again, it is too early to say how this freedom will be used in the United Kingdom, and there is evidence, of Trusts collaborating to set common pay rates (see chapter 5). However, if Trusts do bid up wage levels beyond those prevailing in the rest of the service, there is the possibility of knock-on effects on salaries overall. Equally, decentralisation of pay involves the additional cost of establishing a local negotiating machinery since units will not have had experienced in such bargaining previously. Again, this threatens to produce a further increase in administrative costs. Thus, the costs of quasi-markets must be balanced against any claims that competition will improve efficiency.

*Choice for the Consumer*

Implied in the reforms of health, community care and higher education is the claim that for too long services have been run for the convenience of staff rather than patients, clients and students; the intention is to reverse this by making the needs of the consumers a central concern. Yet under a quasi-market consumers are not in a position to influence the resources allocated to a service directly as health, higher education and community care services will continue to be provided within cash-limited budgets. These in turn, will restrain consumer choice – a point noted by the Social Services Committee in analysing the reforms of both the NHS and Community Care (Social Services Committee 1989: para. 4.37; 1990: para. 4).

An additional factor in limiting consumer choice within the new structures will be the pattern of decision-making that is envisaged. This has two aspects: the exercise of choice via proxies – DHAs, GPs, care managers; or centralised purchasing agencies such as PCFC and the UFC; and the contractual relationships which will link purchasers and providers.

*Whose Choice?*

Under section 46(2) of the NHS and Community Care Act, local authorities are required to consult with health authorities, voluntary organisations, users and carers as to future service provision. Harrison and Wistow's (1992) research in a small number of DHAs found that their respondents were all conscious of the importance of a high level of contact between purchaser and public (Harrison and Wistow 1992: 128). However, consultation and seeking public opinion are not to be confused with services driven by consumer choice.

One of the reasons this will not happen is budgetary constraints and their relationship to the hybrid role of the purchaser. The purchaser role is defined as one of responding to consumers/service users, but also of staying within budgetary limits and, in many cases, an associated task is the enforcement of unit cost reductions on providers. These tensions can be illustrated by looking at two examples: one from the sphere of community care, the other from higher education.

In the Practice Guidance issued to accompany 'Caring for People' it is argued that care management is based on a needs-led approach, which involves 'a shift of influence from those providing to those purchasing services' (Department of Health 1991a: para. 3.7). The purchasers are, of course, the care managers. Care packages are to be agreed with users, carers and other relevant agencies 'to meet identified needs within the care resources available' (ibid.: para. 3.9). The report by the Department of Health and Price Waterhouse, *Implementing Community Care: Purchaser, Commissioner and Provider Roles* talks about the facilitating of 'increased client choice through the empowerment of care managers (though it is important to remember that empowerment of care managers on behalf of clients does not mean absolute choice. Professional views, department policy, budgetary constraints and availability will all have a major impact on the package of care provided)' (Department of Health/Price Waterhouse 1991b: 7). Similarly, the government has announced its intention to oblige local authorities to offer to place people in a home of their choice but 'subject to certain reasonable conditions including limitations on cost' (Department of Health 1992a: para 38).

The significance of such constraints is magnified if the circumstances in which the community care reforms developed are recalled. A major consideration was to end a demand-led policy, i.e. to abolish the open-ended social security subsidy to consumers of residential care in the private and voluntary sector. Thus, it has been pointed out that the reforms will restrain consumer choice and reduce financial empowerment (Laing 1991).

A parallel instance arises in the case of higher education. Under PCFC practice an apparent 'consumerist' aspect is that one of the criteria to be used to assess bids is to be their implications for the 'quality' of provision. However, a major element in the move to a quasi-market in this sector was the desire to increase participation in higher education within a constrained budget and this policy exerted an influence on the role of price in bid assessment.

The fact that PCFC sees these goals as potentially contradictory can be seen in the advice given to Programme Advisory Groups: 'Where the nature of an institution's bid is such as to raise doubts about the ability to provide adequately for the numbers implied and where the strategic plan or other supporting documentation from the institution offers no further explanation, groups should request that officers seek further information from the institution' (cited in Pratt and Hiller 1992: 22). This suggests that a sufficiently low bid could be suspect from the quality standpoint. However, the whole assumption underlying the bidding process is that, in general, cutting resources per student will not compromise quality. Indeed, another aspect of the bidding process allows a programme group to accept a higher price bid if the institution can show its provision is of 'outstanding quality'. Given the general emphasis on reducing unit costs, such bids are marginal to the whole system. Yet, if this policy is to be sustained, it must, presumably, operate on the assumption that, for the institution concerned to maintain the 'quality' of its provision, it will require the resources which its higher price allows it to command. Yet, if this is so, it appears to amount to an admission that forcing down the unit of resource – the major emphasis of policy – *will* compromise quality.

## Contracts and Choice

Purchasing power will be vested in DHAs, GP fund holders, social services departments or, in higher education, centralised purchasing agencies and the relationship between them and the providers of services will be based on contracts. These can take one of three forms: block contracts, which give the purchaser access to a defined range of services for an annual fee; cost and volume contracts whereby the provider receives a sum of money in respect of a certain level of activity defined in terms of a given number of treatments, cases or students enrolled; cost per case contracts that are used to fund referrals that do not fall into either of the previous types of contract (this form would not operate in higher education). The last type is the contractual form which would offer the maximum consumer choice, but is one that neither purchasers nor providers are likely to favour, the former because of the high transaction costs, the latter because it would not guarantee the level of funding. As the Working Paper on Contracts for Health Services states, no DHA would commit itself to pay for a large number of contracts in this way because it 'would risk losing all control over expenditure and its priorities for health care' (Department of Health 1990a: para. 3.40). A similar point is made in the Prachce Guidelines for Community Care (Department of Health 1991a: para. 4.61).

Thus purchasers and providers are most likely to be linked via block and cost, and volume contracts. The marginalisation of the service user in this form of contract relationship has been the subject of comment from important voluntary sector bodies. Age Concern, in its evidence to the Social Services Committee, expressed a concern that 'The element of "choice" for the user will be related to arrangements made by health and local authorities which may have little to do with individuals' perceptions of their own needs' (Social Services Committee 1990: para. 21).

Clearly then, the quasi-market reforms give little direct power to consumers; purchasers, while ostensibly acting on their behalf, will do so within budgetary constraints and forms of contractual relationship, which put cost reduction at the top of the agenda.

*Competing Providers?*

A feature of competitive market models is the freedom of suppliers to enter and exit from those markets: new firms enter, and if they prosper, expand; while unsuccessful firms leave the market. Given the capital cost of entering (and exiting from) the health and education markets, a cost for which government is primarily responsible, an expansion (or contraction) of suppliers is unlikely. Competition, in so far as it takes place, will be between existing institutions. However, with community care, local authorities will be required 'to promote the development of a flourishing independent sector' (Department of Health 1989d: para. 1.11), and will be expected 'to make clear in their community care plans what steps they will be taking to make increased use of non-statutory providers or, where such providers are not currently available, how they propose to stimulate such activity' (ibid.: para. 3.45). Yet, local authorities have not been given any indications as to how they can perform this task. The Policy Guidance accompanying the White Paper does not go beyond reiterating the commitment to a plurality of providers and exhorting Social Services Departments (SSDs) to 'develop strategies which will enable them to provide appropriate information and a supportive climate in order to encourage and facilitate the creation of new services by private and voluntary sector providers' (Department of Health 1990b: para. 4.15). Flynn and Common, in their paper 'Contracts for Community Care', commissioned by the Department of Health, state that 'It should not be assumed that there are alternative suppliers waiting to enter the market...It is likely to be necessary to generate the supply of services if authorities wish to make towards contracting and then continue with a discussion alternative management structures' (Flynn and Common 1990: 25). Research by Wistow et al. of twenty-four LASSDs preparing for their new role found that 'most were only beginning to consider the development of a mixed economy (Wistow et al. 1992: 29). However, the need to develop alternative providers takes on a more immediate significance with the Department of Health's requirement that seventy five per cent of the special transitional community care grant must be spent in the independent sector (Department of Health 1992a: Annex C para. 3).

These injunctions to stimulate a wide range of providers and provision raise a major issues concerning the practicability of such a project.

*Private Provision*

Although the private provision of care has become increasingly significant throughout the 1980s, its efforts have been concentrated in the area of residential/nursing-home care for the elderly. In 1990, the private sector provided 59 per cent of all residential places, compared to 35 per cent in 1981 (Central Statistical Office 1992: 142). However, it cannot be assumed that the sector will continue to grow in this dramatic way. Its structure makes its response to the community care initiative uncertain. In the United Kingdom the corporate sector in 1989 provided only 2.1 per cent of homes for elderly people and 3.7 per cent of places (Lapsley and Llewellyn 1992: 105). The sector is overwhelmingly dominated by small businesses run by owner-managers, exercising personal control over all aspects of the business. Thus, decisions to expand are highly individual and, as Lapsley and Llewellyn point out, 'therefore difficult to predict with any accuracy' (ibid.: 104). Financial viability is obviously relevant. The availability of subsidies in the form of social security payments (increasing from £10 million in 1979 to £1 billion in 1989) had contributed to the rapid expansion (Laing 1991: 6). Indeed, it was argued that many homeowners had made substantial profits from this DSS funding. Lapsley and Llewellyn, in their study of thirty homes in Scotland, found this not to be the case. Rather, many were in financial difficulties as a result of high interest rates and operating on the margins of financial viability (Lapsley and Llewellyn 1992). The changes in the funding arrangements introduced in 1993 mean that local authorities now perform the role of gatekeeper for access to any publicly funded residential care. This may reduce the attractiveness of the sector even further. This example also has interesting implications for the role of the purchaser. Lapsley and Llewellyn found that the financial viability of the homes in their survey was significantly related to the length of time the business had been operating, and that costs of debt service in particular were severe in the early years such that businesses would experience a period of particular vulnerability in this period (ibid.: 108). This suggests that, if a new residential home is providing a reasonable standard of care at an acceptable cost, the purchaser should consider supportive policies. Lapsley and Llewellyn state that 'case managers would perhaps be advised to offer promising new entrants...a long-term contract which might stabilise the position of the home and its elderly residents' (ibid.: 110). In the circumstances there is a good case for such an approach; indeed, it could be argued that it is essential as a means of protecting the interests of vulnerable groups but what is striking is that this sort of co-operative approach is at variance with the arm's length relationship between purchaser and provider, which is central to competitive market models. Another variant of the same issue arises with respect to voluntary sector provision.

*Voluntary Provision*

'Local authority social service departments will develop an increasingly contractual relationship with providers. Contracts will require clear specifications,be enforceable in law, by or against the parties concerned and be one means of safeguarding services' (Department of Health 1990b: paras. 4.23–4.25). Although such relationships between social service departments and voluntary organisations are not a new phenomenon; they have not been extensively used, being reserved for service provision by the private sector (Booth 1990).

The White Paper presents a positive picture of the contractual relationship between local authorities and voluntary organisations, arguing that it will serve 'to clarify the role of voluntary agencies; give them a sounder financial basis and allow them a greater degree of certainty in planning for the future, and enhance the development of more flexible and cost-effective forms of non-statutory provision' (Department of Health 1989d: para. 3.4.12).

In evaluating such claims it is important to bear in mind that the voluntary sector is highly diverse and the very use of the term presumes a coherence and homogeneity which does not in fact exist. In principle, the variation in size and formality of voluntary organisations could be seen as a strength, which a quasi-market might tap. Diversity could thus operate not just to give a range of providers, but also a range of forms of provision.

However, many voluntary organisations are apprehensive about the potential impact of the contract culture. Rather than enhancing their role, they believe that this form of funding could inhibit their distinctive contribution. It is likely that contracts will have a differential impact on the voluntary sector. Given the formality of contracts, they are more likely to be used with large organisations that have an established relationship with local authorities, are bureaucratically organised and employ paid staff. Such groups will be in a position to subsidise contract prices, having income from other sources, monitor the contracts and finance the costs of the contracting process, all of which are attractive features to local authorities viewing contracts within the context of 'value for money' initiatives. The problem was registered in the White Paper where it was stated: 'It will be important to allow scope for the emergence of new, small scale groups and to avoid the over predominance of large, well established voluntary bodies' (Department of Health 1989d: para. 3.4.14). Yet it offered no guidance on how small, informal groups could be preserved. Nor did it appreciate that contractual funding could have a disproportionate impact, for example, on Black and ethnic organisations, which are often small and organised on a self-help basis (Johnson 1991; Qaiyoom 1992) and reverse the growth of this sector which had taken place in the 1980s (Connelly 1990).

Further, it could be argued that contract funding is likely to bias the activities of voluntary organisations. It is suggested that contracts should relate only to service provision while advocacy work should continue to be financed by grants. Given the declining revenue base of local authorities during the 1980s and its expected continuation through the 1990s, two aspects of this division of funding need to be noted. Firstly, even if the political commitment is there, it is less likely that local authorities will be in a position to support advocacy and counselling. Secondly, financial constraints are likely to privilege, even within the contract culture, certain activities over others – those that are regarded as mainstream, rather than marginal.

This bias could also extend to the way in which a voluntary organisation operates. Contracts require legal advice, scrutiny, expertise and knowledge and thus are likely to encourage the employment of paid staff and the professionalisation of management committees. The latter are in the role of employers and thus legally liable if the contract runs into problems. Management committees have always been employers in voluntary organisations, but this role is rarely acknowledged or considered until something goes wrong. The required combination of expert knowledge and legal liability could be a serious problem in attracting lay membership to management committees. Similarly, volunteers who undertake direct service provision to clients could be deterred by the legal constraints which might be imposed on the pattern of service delivery.

The extent to which these effects will materialise in the UK quasi-market for community care services is, still unclear. However, some interesting indications are provided by work undertaken in the United States, where contract relations between government and voluntary organisations are more developed and of longer standing.

## Contracts and the US Voluntary Sector

The process of contracting between government and the voluntary and private sectors has been a significant feature of public service provision in the United States for many years. For example, in Massachusetts, all human services are contracted out and individual states can be contracting for services with over 1,000 different voluntary agencies (Gutch 1992: 73).

Richard Gutch's study, *Contracting Lessons from the US*, based on case studies supplemented by interviews with practitioners in both voluntary and government sectors, academics and researchers, questioned the claimed advantages of contracts for voluntary organisations: for example, that they gave greater security, created longer-term funding arrangements, led to more concern with service outputs and engendered greater equality between the parties. He found that 'One of the most striking features of the US experience of contracting is that none of these advantages appears to have been realised' (ibid.: 74). Most contracts were for one year, involved detailed checking of the costs to be reimbursed and underspending was clawed back; hard-pressed state governments delayed payment and it is estimated that voluntary organisations subsidise contracts by 15–20 per cent, through lower wage rates, longer hours and the substitution of volunteers for paid staff (ibid.: 74).

Voluntary organisations receiving contractual funding expended considerable time accounting for this funding, frequently to different government departments, which required varied reporting formats. One respondent reported that as much as one-third of staff time was spent on paperwork. Thus, this example from the voluntary sector illustrates another dilemma inherent in the purchaser role. Financial restraints impel the purchaser to a more distant relation to the provider and to a reliance on the literal terms of the contract. However, such an approach is likely to narrow the range of both providers and forms of provision. The increasing complexity of contract budgets, the limits on discretion that results from contracts plus the potential problems of personal liability have led to a reduction in the role of volunteer management boards, with volunteers being replaced by professionals, business people (ibid.: 76).

Gutch notes the differential impact of contracts on the independence of the voluntary sector. Those groups with multiple sources of funding and/or a virtual monopoly of supply were better able to resist distortion of their objectives than smaller groups which were more likely to be dependent on a single source of funds (ibid.: 76). Limits to the campaigning work of organisations was most likely to stem from the time constraints of managing a number of different contracts which became 'a further occupation' (ibid.: 76).

Gutch asked his interviewees to speculate about the future role of voluntary organisations in the contract culture. There was a consensus on the future shape of the voluntary sector, with respondents maintaining that a polarised system would emerge: large organisations pursuing a range of strategies such as take-overs and mergers to avoid competition and the development of smaller organisations concentrating on campaigning. Thus the medium and smaller-sized providers would disappear (ibid.: 81). They also noted that as voluntary organisations became more professional, focusing on clients who could afford to pay for services, then the distinctions between voluntary organisations and private organisations would become increasingly blurred (ibid.: 81). An obvious implication of this would be the increasing difficulty of defending the tax allowances of the former.

Gutch's study, based as it is on a number of case studies and interviews, can offer no more than insights into the potential impact of the contract culture on voluntary organisations in the United Kingdom. It does, however,suggest that contracting could change the structures, functions and rationale of the voluntary sector over the next decade.

## Quasi-Markets: Dilemmas and Contradictions

Quasi-markets are distinct from markets encountered in most areas of the private sector in that they will be publicly financed and required to achieve public sector goals. The latter would include, for example, ensuring access to health care on equal terms for the population as a whole, guaranteeing an adequate future supply of doctors and dentists, or ensuring that the higher education system provides places in subjects like applied science or engineering. Attempts to reconcile these goals and conditions set by government with market mechanisms are inherently problematic and are likely to require government intervention and the development of regulatory frameworks. In this section instances of this tension are analysed.

## GP Fund Holders: the Imperatives of Equity

In the introduction to 'Working for Patients', it is argued that the goal of equity, in the sense of universal access to the service on the basis of medical need, will be retained in the new structure. Such a commitment to a traditional public sector objective was likely to lead to tensions with the market-oriented approach of the reforms. This surfaced very quickly in the case of GP fund holders (GPFH).

In addition to providing primary care for their patients, GPFH would also receive a budget to meet the cost of defined inpatient and outpatient services and diagnostic investigations. This budget also covers prescribing by the practice, staffing and accommodation costs. The government believed that practice budgets would offer GPs a number of advantages: an opportunity to improve the quality of services to their patients, stimulation to hospitals to be more responsive to the needs of GPs and patients; encouragement to doctors to develop their practices and to contribute to the way in which NHS money is used to provide services (Department of Health 1989c: para. 1.2). Thus GPFH would be acting as purchasers and competing with DHAs in the placing of contracts.

Some of the first wave of fund holders negotiated with provider units to give their patients shorter waiting times than those applying for patients treated under contract to Districts (Health Committee 1991: para. 92). It was claimed that the fund holders were creating a two-tier system. For example, the general manager of City and Hackney Health Authority claimed, 'This does mean that the question of equity has gone out the window – but this is the reality of GPs building their own practice for elective work. If we do not respond they will spend their money elsewhere' (Millar 1991: 16). This was rejected by fund holders, who saw their role as 'working positively with providers to jack up standards for all GPs (ibid.) and researchers, who argued that GP fund-holding was not creating but merely exposing the inequalities that already existed in the system, and thus was a spur to planners and purchasers to address the problems (Scheuer and Robinson 1991). However, such was the concern of the government that, in June 1991, the Secretary of State for Health announced guidance which was to operate from April 1992. The guidance reiterated that clinical need was to be paramount by requiring that provider units operate common waiting lists for urgent and seriously ill patients, and that the units should not offer contracts to a purchaser which will disadvantage the patients of other purchasers. (There is some confusion over whether fund holders can claim faster treatment for patients if they create additional capacity; Health Committee 1991: paras. 93–6.) Here is a clear example of where the government intervened to limit the effects of the competitive structure which it had introduced. In this case the demands of equity take precedence over the logic of the market. Analogous issues concerning an unwillingness to accept the potential impact of competition is provided by the case of hospital provision in London.

*The London Problem*

The problems of hospital provision in London are of long standing (King's Fund 1992). They involve a number of related facets: despite the use of RAWP funding since the 1970s, 'London retains relatively more acute hospitals than other parts of England' (Beardshaw 1991: para. 5); equally, many hospitals are single-speciality acute units, which are less economic than provision through a single-site District General Hospital (O'Meara 1992: 19); there is a substantial representation of teaching hospitals, which are unevenly spread between Districts. The combination of overprovision, fragmented provision and a large number of teaching hospitals plus higher London labour costs simply means that the costs of providing services in London, especially in Inner London, are substantially higher than elsewhere. According to Calum Paton, Enthoven, whose *Reflections on the Management of the National Health Service* was influential in forming the quasi-market proposals, regarded the internal market as a means of ensuring that centres of excellence, particularly in the capital, would be able to survive financially in that as importers of patients *they* would be able to charge purchasers directly rather than *Districts* doing so, being directly reimbursed for these cross-boundary flows (Paton 1992: 97). However, the NHS reforms have merely served to highlight and exacerbate the problems of the London hospitals.

The development of a quasi-market in health care has three distinct impacts on this question: the logic of the purchaser/provider split; the effect of capital charges; and the impact of the system of funding of Districts.

As has been indicated throughout this chapter, a key feature in the development of quasi-markets has been the attempt to reduce, or at least control, costs. With the purchaser/provider split, London hospitals will have to compete between themselves and with others outside the capital. At the same time, purchasers have incentives to seek out lower-cost providers to increase the number of cases which can be treated from their budget. This clearly is designed to put pressure on higher-cost suppliers. This tendency is strengthened by another important innovation in the quasi-market in health: the introduction of capital charges. Prior to the quasi-market units were not charged in any form for the capital assets which they used. However, under the quasi-market units have to meet a depreciation and an interest charge. In the case of directly managed units, for example, such payments are made directly to Region. In order to meet such capital charges units must incorporate them into their contract prices.

The system is working with a *transitional* period in which Districts, when placing their contracts, are funded in line with the capital charges of the provider units which they have historically used. Thus, in this period a provider unit with high capital charges should not be disadvantaged since the District is funded to pay such charges. However, *after* this transitional period Districts will be funded on the basis of the *national average* for capital charges. Naturally, this will mean that the District has a marked disincentive to use a provider with high capital charges and hence high costs since now its funding does not cover such costs. Consequently, capital charges could *inter alia* operate to make it difficult for units with high capital charges to survive.

This is particularly pertinent to London for two reasons: on average, capital charges per episode in London are relatively high; for example, in 1990 the Inner London average was £332 as against £209 for the rest of the Thames area (Akehurst et al. 1991). In addition, there are sharp variations between *units* within London: for example, in 1991 the Central Middlesex Hospital was estimated to have a capital charge per patient stay of £690, while the figure for the Greenwich hospital was £290 (O'Meara 1992: 36).

**Table 3.1** Estimated percentage of non-maternity, non-psychiatric cases treated in NHS teaching districts in London, who are normally resident outside the District, 1986

| Teaching DHA | % |
| --- | --- |
| Paddington & North Kensington | 58.5 |
| Riverside | 52.1 |
| Hampstead | 69.3 |
| Bloomsbury | 84.6 |
| City & Hackney | 63.0 |
| Tower Hamlets | 46.8 |
| West Lambeth | 65.3 |
| Camberwell | 42.3 |
| Lewisham & North Southwark | 46.3 |
| Wandsworth | 55.0 |

*Source*: Adapted from The Social Services Select Committee (1989 para. 128)

The third part of the London problem concerns the funding of the District Health Authorities. London hospitals have traditionally always had a very large number of non-residents, a feature illustrated in Table 3.1. However, from 1 April 1991, the funding of Districts has been based on the size of the resident population and the use that this population had made of services in the past. Thus health authorities covering Inner London found themselves stripped of funds because of their relatively small residential populations and through the loss of money they had previously automatically received by treating patients from outside their boundaries, from health authorities where the patients lived. The move to weighted capitation could further reduce the purchasing power of these authorities (Ham 1991: 3). Thus, even if the London health authorities wished to support 'their own hospitals', they will find it increasingly difficult to do so. As the Third Report from the Health Committee commented: 'There is no question that left to its own devices, the operation of the internal market is likely to deal with the problem of over capacity in London' (The Health Committee 1991: para. 79).

However, rather than allow this to happen, the government intervened. In the first year of the quasi-market, health authorities were actively discouraged by the Department of Health from using their budgets 'entrepreneurially', they were exhorted to maintain a steady state in placing their contracts. Towards the end of the year the government took two other interventionist steps: it established the Tomlinson Committee to consider the balance of health needs and health provision in the capital; then it ordered the Thames health regions to set aside 1 per cent of their budget for 1992–3 to keep the London hospitals afloat (*The Guardian*, 23 January 92). If, when and how the government decides to act on recommendations of the Tomlinson Report, namely a reduction of 2,500 beds in London, the closure of St Bartholomew's and Middlesex Hospitals, the merger of Guy's and St Thomas's and other specialist hospitals – it will be accepting that the provision in London cannot be left to the market (Department of Health 1992b).

*Regulating the Market: Controlling the Entrepreneur*

Establishing quasi-markets is likely to create a series of financial incentives to purchasers and providers, which did not exist under the pre-market system. In principle, such financial incentives are designed to be linked to improvements in service provision. However, there are various instances in which strategies to generate revenue can be divorced from, or even compromise, service standards. This can be illustrated in the case of health care.

With the GP fund-holding scheme, any surplus generated on the budget does not go directly into the fundholder's pocket, but must be ploughed back into the practice. Arguably, however, there is an indirect incentive here for GPs to change their behaviour, in that, in future, capitation payments are to be of increased significance in the pattern of payment of GPs. Thus, any surplus could be used to increase income and develop additional facilities with the object of attracting new patients by offering a wider range of services. This seems a positive use of this new power but the downside is that tactics might be used to ensure that a surplus is increased. Three alternatives are worth considering here. First, GPFH might be more careful in their selection of patients, preferring the 'good risks'. Second, they could under-refer patients to hospitals. Third, they could delay sending patients to hospital until they had to be admitted as Accident and Emergency (A and E) cases. In such cases the costs fall on the DHA (Ham 1992: 23). Such tactics help the GPFH to increase their budget surplus but are all practices which could compromise standards of health care.

The Eighth Report of the Social Services Committee had recognised that, while health care provision would operate in a context of contracts agreed between purchasers and providers, quasi-markets gave 'considerable scope for the entrepreneurial hospital manager or clinician to bring in additional work into the hospital,for which the hospital would be remunerated' (Social Services Committee 1989: para. 2.68). The Committee referred to several ways of doing this: admitting patients who present themselves at A and E departments and thus billing the District (ibid.: para. 2.63); once a patient has been admitted doing more for them than the hospital might otherwise have done, in the knowledge that the costs would be reimbursed (ibid.: para. 2.69); many teaching hospitals had consultants with joint appointments with other hospitals and other Districts and would be able to refer patients to their own hospitals as a tertiary referral with the teaching hospital billing the DHA (ibid.: para. 2.10).

Although, it could be objected that this discussion by the Social Services Committee was purely theoretical, examples of such organisational ploys already in use in the reformed NHS have quickly come to light. The following instances are cited by a Director of Purchasing in the NHS: ensuring that, if possible, a patient did not give a local address but a more distant one, so that, if admission was necessary, it would be financed as an extra-contractual referral; billing the purchaser for the actual cost of procedures, although this may be more than they had agreed to pay, in the hope that they might not notice the difference; discharging a patient before the conclusion of treatment but planning a readmission, thus allowing the unit to charge for two admissions; finally, attempts could be made to direct patients away from casualty departments (where costs are borne by the provider units) to an emergency admission, which attracted the full speciality costs of the bed to which the patient was admitted (Anonymous 1992: 25). All these are examples of 'gaming' to generate increased revenue. The extent of such practices and the regulatory problems which they pose can be seen in a more developed form if we look at US experience.

## Competition and Regulation: Lessons from the United States

Between 1945 and the mid-1970s access to medical care in the United States expanded rapidly, with the growth of private insurance coverage, frequently offered as a benefit of employment, and the introduction in the 1960s of Medicare (a federally funded programme for people over 65) and Medicaid (an insurance scheme for low-income families funded jointly by federal and state governments) (Quam 1989: 114). In all cases the most common form of finance was retrospective reimbursement. Patients were billed for medical servies but payment came retrospectively from third parties – private insurers, the Federal government and state governments. The incentive to high costs with this system was straightforward. Since reimbursement was retrospective, the providers of medical services were assured of getting their bills paid and this created an obvious incentive to increase services to the patient. As the patients did not pay directly, they had no incentive to restrain the supply of the service and the accompanying cost. Expenditure on health care escalated from 5.9 per cent of GNP in 1965 to 9.1 per cent in 1980 (Robinson 1990: 19).

A major attempt to contain health care costs was the development of prospective reimbursement systems. An important example of this is where a fixed rate per case is set in advance of treatment for a given range of diagnostic categories. The system aims to generate an incentive to more economical treatment since, as the rate is set prospectively, costly treatment procedures involve the provider in absorbing the difference between the cost and the prospective rate as a loss (Hollingsworth 1986: 155)

The most ambitious scheme of this kind was the one introduced in New Jersey, and in 1983, Medicare moved to a similar form of reimbursement. Payment in both schemes was determined by allocating the patients to one of 467 Diagnostic Related Groups (DRGs), each of which reflected a like use of resources. DRGs were subsequently adopted by private insurers. Essentially DRGs were a means of exerting control over costs.

However, as hospitals believed that DRGs threatened their income they resorted to a number of strategies to maintain or increase their revenues. There was an incentive to increase the number of admissions as this generated more income. Between 1979 and 1984, New Jersey hospitals increased admissions per capita by more than 6 per cent, while admissions were declining 5 per cent nationally (Weiner et al. 1987: 469). However, the most notorious strategy used to maintain or expand revenue was to allocate a patient to the highest applicable diagnostic category, a feature known as 'DRG creep' (Simborg 1981). DRG rates set a given fee for a particular diagnostic category. However, specific illnesses do not fall into simple self-contained categories, as they involve combinations of conditions and thus primary and secondary diagnoses. For payment purposes the DRG rate depends on the primary diagnosis. Weiner compared twelve pairs of high-volume DRGs – the simple diagnosis and the same diagnosis with complications. Following the introduction of DRGs in 1981, the New Jersey State Department of Health reported a dramatic shift in the volume of cases from the simple to the complicated diagnosis between 1981 and 1984. The estimated revenue gain from this change in case mix was $38.7 million, or $380,000 per hospital (ibid.: 470). The response by almost all third party payers and insurers has been the introduction of some form of utilisation review of clinical activity (Ermann 1988). In the case of Medicare this is Peer Review Organisation, whereby doctors are monitored through audits of their medical practice and this is then compared to standards of practice developed by their peers (Weiner and Ferris 1990: 17).

The discussion of DRGs is relevant to the NHS since it shows how a cost-control technique using simple economic mechanisms can be manipulated, and that to combat this resources have to be deployed into regulation.

*Monitoring Quality*

While quasi-markets require a regulatory structure to deal with problems of gaming, a further regulatory issue which is becoming increasingly salient is the attempt to control standards of 'quality'. Government is often prone to cite the private sector as a model with respect to standards of quality. This would suggest that quality issues could be effectively left to purchasers and providers. However, what is striking is that additional layers of central control are being superimposed to secure quality.

In the mixed economy of care, the Department of Health will play an important part in helping to maintain and improve the quality of care provided: it will require each local authority, under section 46 of the NHS and Community Care Act to prepare a Community Care Plan, the contents of which are closely prescribed: for example, the procedures to be used in assessing the needs of the population, the client groups for whom services are to be arranged and how issues of quality are to be handled. In particular, the plans must state the steps to be taken to ensure quality in the purchasing and provision of services (for example, building in quality standards to contracts and service specifications) and how this is to be monitored. Each local authority must also establish a complaints procedure to provide 'an effective means of allowing service users...to complain about the quality or nature of social services' (Department of Health 1990b: para. 6.10). Inspection units are to be set up as a means of checking and promoting the quality of services, initially in residential care and subsequently in all sectors. The Department will use its Social Services Inspectorate to inspect plans and monitor the arrangements put in place by SSDs to 'ensure quality of service provision' (ibid.: para. 2.20).

While not being quite so prescriptive in the area of health there is little indication that quality is to be left to be determined by competitive mechanisms. Both RHAs and DHAs are to assume a role in ensuring quality. Regions are to concentrate on setting performance criteria, monitoring the performance of the Health Service and evaluating its effectiveness (Department of Health 1989a: para. 2.7). Districts must ensure 'that their population has access to a comprehensive range of high quality...services' (ibid.: para. 2.11). As with community care, contracts will be required to include quality specifications. Medical audit will address the 'critical analysis of the quality of medical care' (Department of Health 1989: para. 5.3), and the Audit Commission will have responsibility for the statutory audit of health authorities.

Parallel developments have occurred in higher education. Thus, HMI reports are to be a key source for PCFC in determining whether bids claiming provision of 'outstanding quality' are sound.

Thus central direction and bureaucratic structures are summoned to perform a task which one might have expected, given the government's ideological stance, to be left to markets. This paradox requires an explanation. Concerns over quality are in many respects a function of the pressures on all the services covered to increase throughput without corresponding increases in resources. Reference to quality is frequently juxtaposed to slogans like the need to promote 'value for money' and 'cost-effective services' giving rise to the suspicion that, for the government, quality is a smokescreen for the decline in the standards of services which will follow from attempts to squeeze more out of existing resources. The existence of quality systems will be used to counter claims that standards are falling: after all such systems are in place to prevent *that* occurring.

## Conclusion

Quasi-markets were introduced as an alternative to full-scale privatisation of welfare services. While the services would continue to be publicly funded, they would be provided by competing units within the public sector but also from the private and voluntary sectors. It was claimed that quasi-markets would stimulate efficiency, enhance consumer choice and encourage diversity through competition between providers. However, such markets generate contradictory pressures and as such it is not possible to sustain all the claims which are made for them. In particular, it is difficult to reconcile consumer choice with budgetary constraints; efficiency with the increase in administrative and transaction costs; competition with new forms of regulation. Equally, political objectives – commitment to equity, access, accountability for the use of resources – sit uneasily with the effects of market mechanisms. In the 1990s they are likely to function in a context where the dual pressures of cost containment and for 'performance' via increased throughput will operate. These will be reinforced by the emphasis on targets in the *Citizen's Charter*. Such pressures are likely to push quasi-markets in a definite direction which privileges certain objectives at the expense of others.

# 4

## Competitive Tendering: the Case of the Vanishing Producers

An important development in the framework within which public-sector services are managed in the United Kingdom has been the introduction of Compulsory Competitive Tendering (CCT). This policy has, from the outset, generated controversy, but it is important to stress that the debate is not just one about pros and cons but also one that involves the question of how CCT is characterised. On the political left CCT has been seen as an illegitimate and authoritarian policy, which has sought to impose an alien set of practices on democratically elected local government. In contrast, CCT has also been seen as a neutral management technique which has no political implications. Thus, a *Financial Times* leader of 26 November 1986 refers to CCT as 'a microeconomic search for efficiency which has little to do with ideology' (cited in Cubbin et al. 1987: 56). In a similar vein the Audit Commission sees a simple parallel between decisions on contracting out in business and in local authorities:

> The decision to 'make or buy' goods and services is among the most important facing any commercial undertaking. Local authorities face precisely similar choices between providing services directly or buying them in from outside suppliers...The choice between providing a service directly and buying it in should be based on management's assessment of which route will derive the most cost competitive service in the long run. (Audit Commission 1987: 1).

The thesis developed in this chapter is that arguments of the latter form are untenable. It seeks to demonstrate that any evaluation of CCT cannot be divorced from the fact that it is a policy that necessarily involves fundamental political choices and reference to central political values. The argument is divided into four sections: the first examines the defining features of the policy and gives an outline history of the development of the policy in the British context; the second discusses the regulatory framework within which the policy has operated and its underlying rationale; the third looks at the impact of the policy in terms of whether it has generated 'savings' and its significance for conditions of employment in the areas covered,this section draws not just on British experience but also utilises evidence on the effects of parallel practices in the United States; the final section discusses the political choices involved in the evaluation of CCT.

## CCT and Privatisation

It has become a common practice to see CCT as part of a general trend towards privatisation. However, this runs the risk of obscuring certain distinctive features of the policy. Central to the UK privatisation programme has been the sale, in whole or in part, of major public assets such as British Telecom (BT), British Gas (BG) and the electricity industry. This has been a complex procedure since it has usually involved the establishment by government of a regulatory framework within the privatised industry operates. The regulatory framework means that in a certain areas the companies concerned do not have a completely free hand in determining company policy. In the case of BT and BG, pricing policy is regulated and the government holds what is termed a 'golden share', which enables it to exert control over decisions such as disposal of assets and share issues (Marsh 1991: 464). Even so, there is a privatisation of both *provision* as the service is now provided by a private sector firm and of *finance* since, within the constraints imposed by regulation, the firm can set prices and raise capital in the form it regards as appropriate.

In contrast, competitive tendering (CT) is a process whereby services currently provided by public sector suppliers are put out to tender. This usually involves a bid by an in-house public sector supplier which is compared to bids from outside contractors (usually private sector but, in some cases, from the voluntary sector). With CT the planning and finance functions remain public (Ascher 1987: 7). Thus, a local authority which introduces CT will continue to decide what level of service it wishes to provide (e.g. the number of times refuse is collected per week) and specify features of how the service will be provided (e.g. whether refuse will be collected from the side of the road or the back of the house). The service continues to be publicly financed, being paid for predominantly out of a combination of central and local government taxation, although this does not exclude the use of direct charges.

The effect of CT *may* be that service provision moves from public to private sector. The public sector provider or Direct Labour Organisation (DLO) might be unsuccessful in its bid and hence lose the contract. However, the shift is not necessarily permanent. Contracts have been awarded for fixed periods to a contractor but the contact has been returned 'in-house' in a subsequent round of bidding. (For an interesting case study, which is discussed later in the chapter, see Bach 1989). If a DLO is successful it is referred to as a Direct Service Organisation or DSO (Lapsley and Llewellyn 1991: 43).

CT should be distinguished from contracting out. CT involves a regular competition between public and outside suppliers. In contrast, a policy of contracting out involves closing down the public sector provision and relying on outside contractors for the future provision of the service (Treasury 1986: 15). In such cases a genuine privatisation of *provision* operates, though planning and finance remains public. Finally, CT is distinct from procurement. All public sector bodies buy in goods and services on a substantial scale from outside suppliers, but procurement cases relate to goods or services which have never been produced in-house (purchase of motor vehicles is an obvious example). In contrast, the services covered by CT like refuse collection or street cleaning have usually been provided in-house but the tendering process opens the possibility of a shift in provision (Ascher 1987: 136). CCT is sometimes treated as a form of quasi-market. This is perfectly legitimate in that it involves two defining features of such markets, public funding and the purchaser/provider split. However, we have opted to treat it as a distinct form for two reasons: because it involves conditions on the form of contract and criteria for tender assessment, imposed by central government, which are more detailed than those that apply in the quasi-markets discussed in chapter 3: in addition, it raises issues about the treatment of producer groups in a particularly pointed form. Both these issues are discussed in detail later in the chapter.

## Compulsory Competitive Tendering: the Genesis of a Policy

Competitive tendering *per se* refers to a policy initiated by the public body involved. In contrast CCT means that an *obligation* is being imposed to use competitive tendering for a range of services and that such tendering operates within a regulatory framework. As will be argued later, the compulsory element has a number of crucial ramifications in assessment of this policy.

Throughout the 1980s CCT evolved in a series of developments at the level of central government departments. (for a summary see Treasury 1991: Annex). However, the most interesting developments have occurred in local government and in the National Health Service (NHS). The first major development came in the Local Government and Land Act 1980. This legislation imposed an obligation on local authorities to introduce tendering for building construction and maintenance of buildings and highways (Walsh 1989: 36). However, the impact of this legislation was limited primarily because of the number of exceptions that were allowed: initially, tendering was not required for building work under £10,000 and work on highways under £100,000; and small DLOs were not covered (ibid.: 37). The effect of these restrictions meant that the impact on DLOs, at least in terms of their share of contract work, was relatively small. Over the period 1982–3 to 1985–6 the DLO share of local authority construction and maintainance work in England and Wales fell only marginally from 43.3 per to 42.6 cent (ibid.).

With respect to the NHS the Conservative 1983 manifesto contained a commitment to introduce CCT for three ancillary services: catering, laundry services and cleaning. This policy was initiated in a DHSS circular HC (83) 18, issued in September 1983. The circular required that, from February 1984, Regional Health Authorities (RHAs) should submit tendering programmes prepared by Districts to the Ministry within two months or furnish an explanation for the failure of Districts to provide such a programme. Similar obligations were imposed on special health authorities and teaching hospitals (DHSS 1983: 2).

A further and much more significant move to introduce CCT in local government came with the Local Government Act 1988. Under this legislation CCT was extended to the following services, provided mainly by local authorities but also by other bodies outside central government, such as development corporations and urban development corporations: refuse collection, building cleaning, other cleaning (mainly street cleaning), catering in education and welfare establishments, grounds maintenance, vehicle maintenance, sports and leisure management (Local Government Act 1988, section 2 (2)).

As far as the 1990s are concerned, there are plans to extend the scope of CCT to cover a range of services previously excluded. So far the services covered have predominantly been support services where the main employee groups involved have been manual staff. In future the plan is to broaden CCT in both central and local government to cover 'professional' services such as the provision of accounting, legal, architectural and personnel services (Treasury 1991: 24). *The Citizen's Charter* extends the list to include management of local authority housing.

## The Regulatory Framework

The imposition of CCT on local and health authorities was accompanied by an elaborate but ambiguous regulatory framework. CCT requires local and health authorities to test in-house suppliers against external competition, but in itself this indicates nothing about the criteria which are to be used to select the winning tender. It is this that is revealed in the fine print of the regulatory framework.

The first striking feature is the dominance of cost criteria. In discussing tender appraisal in the services covered in the NHS circular HC (83) 18 states: 'In no circumstances should a contractor not submitting the lowest tender be awarded the contract unless there are compelling reasons endorsed at District Authority level for taking such a decision.' Almost identical language is contained in the guidance notes on competition procedures under the Local Government Act 1988, issued by the Department of the Environment: 'The Secretary of State believes that a decision to reject a lower bid in favour of the DSO will be consistent with the duty of the authority to avoid restriction, distortion or prevention of competition only if it can be shown that there were sound reasons to justify rejection of the lower tender' (Department of the Environment 1991: 2).

In fact, cost comparisons involve a number of complications since what is central is not the tender price per se but the net saving to the authority. This means that bids will be adjusted by the local authority or health authority to reflect the overall cost implications of either accepting a bid from an external contractor or maintaining the supply in-house. Thus, a lower bid from an outside contractor could involve additional redundancies which will involve corresponding costs for the authority. It is permissible under the Local Government Act (Department of the Environment 1991: 9) and in the NHS (DHSS 1983: Appendix ii) for authorities to to take such costs into account. Conversely, financial resources could be *released* where the contract is won by an outside contractor. An example would be depreciation allowances since, if the service were not provided in-house, the assets concerned would not have to be replaced (Ascher 1987: ch. 5).

What counts as a 'good reason' for rejecting a lower bid is ambiguous. Circular HC (83) 18 states that the authority should only let the contract to the lowest bidder if it 'is satisfied about the ability of the contractor to deliver the service in accordance with contract terms.' (DHSS 1983: Appendix ii). However, there is at least a strong negative injunction spelling out what is not to be taken into account and that is the conditions under which workers are employed by the various bidders.

With respect to the NHS, HC (83) 18 advises that tender documents 'should detail the service requirements, frequencies and standards required. They should not stipulate detailed requirements for staffing,the length of time needed to undertake tasks, supervisors and equipment levels' (DHSS 1983: Appendix i; emphasis in the original).

The requirement not to take into account conditions of employment is stipulated even more explicitly and comprehensively in the Local Government Act 1988. This legislation aims to preclude the authority covered from taking into account various 'non-commercial matters' among which are included contractor terms and conditions of employment; composition of workforce and conduct of contractors in industrial disputes' (Local Government Act 1988: section 17 (5)).

There is a quite explicit political message here. As was argued in chapter 1, a central feature of the New Right was the hostility to producer groups in general and trade unions in particular. Trade unions were attacked as key institutions which offended both the tenets of market economics and the dogma of individualism. A number of links exist between competitive tendering and the relative strength of trade unions. As will be demonstrated later, the process of competitive tendering is regularly associated with job loss whether the contract is won in-house or by an outside contractor. In such circumstances even if a contract is won there is the likelihood that job losses will mean a loss of membership for the trade unions involved. Equally, where contracts are won by outside suppliers they are less likely to recognise trade unions. The 1991 Labour Force Survey includes evidence on relative levels of unionisation by economic sector: the overall level of union density (union members as a percentage of employees) in 1991 was 37 per cent but the public sector included areas where levels of union density were much higher; in local government density was 65 per cent and hospitals 66 per cent. In contrast density in private services was low relative to the overall average, with, for example, density at 9 per cent in business services and 11 per cent in hotels and catering (cited in Labour Research 1992 b: 12 ). This pattern is not unique to the United Kingdom. A study in the United States covering 1,256 cities with a population in excess of 10,000 found that the 29 per cent of private sanitation employees working on public contracts were unionised as against a unionisation rate of 40 per cent for directly publicly employed staff (Chandler and Feuille 1991: 19).

As with the case of employment law (see chapter 1) it is striking how far the formal prohibitions against taking employment conditions into account extend. For example, these restrictions are applied to the disabled. The House of Lords amended the original bill in the case of the

Local Government Bill, to allow authorities to take into account contractor policies on employment for people with disabilities, but this was rejected when the legislation was returned to the Commons (Walsh 1987: 40). However, it is permissible for a local authority to allow for additional costs deriving from employing disabled persons in assessing a tender (Department of the Environment 1991: 2).

The political values embodied in the regulatory regime are thus diametrically opposed to those espoused by, in particular, Labour-controlled local authorities. Not surprisingly then, there has been an attempt to ensure that local authorities do not engage in practices which Conservative governments have seen as having 'the effect of restricting, distorting or preventing competition' (Local Government Act 1988: section 7 (7)). Examples of such practices are 'packaging of contracts so that they are too large so as to deter even fairly large contractors from applying for them' (Department of the Environment 1991: 6); contractors should be selected so as to reflect,'the degree of realistic competition that the DSO was required to face' (Department of the Environment 1991: 8) and this should preclude deliberately short listing contractors with high prices or likely to be unsatisfactory in other respects; authorities are permitted to require 'performance bonds' from contractors which should be related to costs which might be incurred in remedying defects in the work performed, 'excessive' bonds contradict the competitive code and should not exceed 10–15 per cent of the annual contract value (ibid.).

These regulatory powers are underpinned by sanctions. Under section 13 of the 1988 Act those authorities covered can be required to rebut claims that they have infringed the various prohibitions of the Act and under section 14, if the Secretary of State finds the response unsatisfactory,the power is available to specify conditions attached to the work, the most common being to order the authority to re-tender,or even to prohibit the (in-house) supplier from carrying out the work.

## The Operation of the Regulatory Framework

As has already been argued, the emphasis on cost reduction and the pronounced bias against the interests of employees embodied in the legislation on CCT meant that, Labour authorities in particular could be expected to resist it. For example, Kerley and Wynn point out that after the 1988 Act was passed, the Convention of Scottish Local Authorities and the Scottish TUC formed a joint committee to 'formulate joint ground rules by which Scottish Local Authorities and the trade unions could co-operate to minimise the loss of employment and direct services arising from commercial tendering' (Kerley and Wynn 1991: 33).

The whole process of CCT is thus firmly inserted in the conflictual relationship between central government and local authorities which has been a central issue in British politics in the 1980s and promises to continue to be so in the 1990s.

As in all cases of this kind it is difficult to assess the effects of the regulatory powers contained in the 1988 Act. Table 4.1 shows that the powers under sections 13 and 14 have been used sparingly so far with a total of twenty-two cases up to June 1991, and section 14 powers have been used to require re-tendering rather than the prohibition of the DSO carrying out the work concerned.

**Table 4.1** 'Anti-competitive' notices under the Local Government Act 1988 (to June 1991)

| | |
|---|---|
| Total Number of Cases of which | 22 |
| Section 13 notices | 11 |
| Section 14 notices | 11 |
| Outcomes of Section 13 notices: | |
| No further action | 7 |
| Re-tender | 1 |
| Not decided | 3 |
| Outcomes of Section 14 Notices: | |
| Re-tender | 10 |
| Not yet decided | 1 |
| Political control of councils subject to section 13 and 14 notices | |
| Labour | 14 |
| Conservative | 4 |
| Independent | 3 |
| Not stated | 1 |

*Source*: Courcouf (1991); *Public Service Action* (February 1991)

The limited use of sanctions does not, of course, imply that the regulatory framework is of no significance. Sanctions may not only be designed *pour encourager les autres* but may actually do so.

In such a politically polarised context a relevant consideration is not just the content of the regulatory framework but also its clarity and coherence. The regulation of CCT in both health and local authorities requires the authority to *disregard* conditions of employment in evaluating tenders. However, there is a fine line between this condition and the requirement that the viability of the contractor's bid should be evaluated. This tension is revealed in a report of a multi-departmental review of competitive tendering and contracting for services in central government departments, published in 1986. On the one hand, the document argues that savings from contracting out derived from contractors offering inferior conditions of employment (Treasury 1986: 33). On the other hand, it repudiates the notion that viability can be assessed without reference to conditions of employment: 'service contracts have to be conducted on the basis of mutual trust because although detailed specification and monitoring are necessary it is difficult to make such contracts entirely comprehensive. It is essential, therefore, to check that the contractor *plans to recruit enough staff and to pay them enough*' (ibid.; our emphasis).

It is also clear that, even amongst authorities which have not resisted CCT, staffing levels have been regarded as a pertinent consideration. A detailed case study by Bach (1989) discusses two rounds of CCT in a new District General Hospital. In this case senior management were sympathetic to CT, a fact that was indicated by an outside contractor winning the contract in the first round of tendering. Five bids were short listed, including the in-house bid, but the lowest bid, which proposed to undertake the contract with a staffing level of 29.37 Whole Time Equivalent (WTE) staff, was rejected in favour of an outside contractor bid with a staffing level of 45.68 WTE on the grounds that the lowest bid was regarded as unviable by management (Bach 1989: 7).

*A Level Playing Field?*

Discussions of CCT have regularly emphasised the pertinence of *competition* in analysing the underlying rationale behind the policy. This is reflected in official documents: The Local Government Act 1988 states that its aim is 'to secure that local and other public authorities undertake certain activities only if they can do so competitively'; similarly circular HC (83) 18 involves the objective of obliging authorities to 'test the cost of their support services' (DHSS 1983: 1). Furthermore, academic commentators have seen the policy as having the object of creating 'contestable markets'. This concept refers to a reorientation of the economic theory of competition during the 1980s (Walsh 1989:46). According to this position the effects of competition are achieved not by the number of actual competitors but rather by the possibility of competitors entering (and thus 'contesting') the markets concerned. In such circumstances, it is argued economic enterprises will operate *as if* they were facing actual competition.

At first sight this *raison d'être* seems to apply CCT. Thus, what it can be claimed to achieve is the break-up of monopoly provision exposing the in-house supplier to the effects of competitive pressures. In turn it is possible to argue that many key elements of the regulatory framework are consistent with such arguments. For instance, the Local Government Act 1988 obliges authorities to advertise the contracts in the local and trade press and make available detailed specifications of the work required (Local Government Act 1988: Section 7 (2)). Equally, the prohibitions on such practices as contract packaging to deter entrants and manipulated shortlists can be seen as part of the object of rendering the sector 'contestable'.

This, equally, seems to imply that the legislation and regulatory framework is designed to create a 'level playing field' on which private- and public-sector suppliers can compete on equal terms. In many fundamental respects, however, this reading of CCT is misleading.

The first significant difference between public and private sector providers is their ability to bid for contracts in the sector in which CCT operates. A private sector supplier is able to bid for any contract put out to tender. In contrast, public sector providers are much more circumscribed in the range of work for which they can tender.

The issue involves a number of complexities and is governed by the Local Authorities (Goods and Services) Act 1970. Under this legislation local authorities were allowed to co-operate with each other to promote 'economy and efficiency'. The Act allows a local authority to supply services to another and does not impose restrictions on the size or financial value of the contracts concerned nor the geographical area in which they may operate. What *is* precluded by the legislation is a situation where the Authority 'engages in trade' by providing services to other authorities which are incidental to their functions as authorities. This might be argued to cover a local authority DSO operating as a specialised contractor analogous to a private sector operator (Macgregor 1991: 61).

The Audit Commission has given a restrictive interpretation to this legislation. It has argued that a local authority may only supply its services to another authority if two conditions are met: it has surplus capacity; and, the majority of the work undertaken by the DSO is for its own authority. This interpretation has been disputed. For example, Macgregor has argued that the logic of the aim of supporting 'economy and efficiency' is to enable two or more authorities to 'create sufficient capacity' in a given area of work (ibid.).

The issue may have significance for two reasons: the limitations on public sector bidders mean that there is an asymmetry between the effects of losing a contract for private- and public sector suppliers. In the former case the loss is likely to *reduce* the volume of business for the enterprise but it remains free to bid for other public and private sector contracts. In the latter case the loss is potentially fatal for the DLO/DSO since its *raison d'être* is removed. This issue is likely to be significant even if a liberal reading of the 1970 Act is used. Thus, Macgregor argues that in legal terms: 'if external work is only sought to sustain an *already* ailing DSO, it must be questionable' (ibid.; emphasis in the original).

The second potential effect relates to the greater scope for private sector suppliers to achieve scale economies via their ability to bid for a range of contracts. Thus, Mcguirk argues that Tyler Environmental Services (a private contractor) is an example of a firm which has achieved savings through sharing facilities by winning contracts, initially in Wandsworth and Sevenoaks, and following up with further wins giving it eleven contracts in adjacent areas on the southern outskirts of London. In contrast, the constraints on DSOs limit such strategies (Mcguirk 1991: 15).

Another difference in the treatment of DSOs and private sector suppliers relate to the conditions imposed in both the Local Government and Planning Act 1980 and the Local Government Act 1988. Under both pieces of legislation DSOs are required to be treated as distinct accounting units and make a 5 per cent return on the capital they employ. It could be argued that the treatment is equitable in that private sector suppliers would also be expected to make positive rates of return. However, the difference is that DSOs could be argued not to be in a position to cross-subsidise while this option *is* available to private sector suppliers. This gives the latter the opportunity to 'loss-lead' on a given contract. However, the significance of this particular feature is debateable. Thus, a recent study of DSOs in Scotland engaged in building work found rates of return which were significantly higher than those attained in private sector construction (Lapsley and Llewellyn 1991: 47–8). Furthermore, the non-availability of cross-subsidy to DSOs can be exaggerated since, it may be possible to load work not covered by CCT with overhead costs and conversely reduced overheads allocated to work covered by tendering.

A more blatant variation in treatment, and one that flatly contradicts 'competition' criteria, relates to the difference in the regulation of contracted-out services and of services provided in-house. The legislation on CCT refers exclusively to services where the authority concerned *wishes to* retain the service in-house. In such a case if the service is covered by the legislation the CT is obligatory. In contrast, no such obligations apply to a policy of *contracting out*. Should a local authority wish simply to terminate public provision and contract out the service to the private sector there is no requirement to test the private sector contractor (Painter 1991: 193).

As was indicated earlier, cost criteria are ascribed a central role in tender evaluation. However, even here there are variations in the rules applied to public and private sector. In some cases this is exemplified in the operation of the regulatory process. Ascher cites two cases of DHSS intervention where cost criteria were applied inconsistently: in the first case a lower cost bid from in-house laundry services was rejected on the grounds that the capital equipment could be used more effectively on other uses while, simultaneously, a cleaning contract was reawarded to a private-sector supplier with the lowest bid in cost terms (Ascher 1987: 186).

The dual standard has now been carried further with the introduction of CCT for white-collar and professional services referred to above. In this case a 180-degree turn has been effected. Thus, an article in the *Financial Times* of 7 October 1991 reports that,'because salary levels for professional staff in local government are generally lower than in the private sector the government believes private companies would not have a fair chance to compete for local authority work.' The same report cites the contracting out of the budget preparation process to Touche Ross by the Conservative-controlled South Oxfordshire District Council. The Touche Ross bid was £28,000, the in-house tender was £15,000. It would clearly be going too far to argue that CCT has nothing to do with competition. However, as with so many areas of policy under Mrs Thatcher and Mr Major economic orthodoxy has been strongly tempered by the dictates of ideology and the social class affected by the measures. The regime applicable to dustmen and cleaners is not to be applied to lawyers and accountants.

*Who Wins the Contracts?*

A central political issue with respect to CCT relates to how far it has resulted in the privatisation of provision. However,it is important to stress that it would be quite wrong to limit any assessment of its impact simply to this issue. The impact of CCT may involve other key changes since, given the regulatory framework, important variations in the terms and conditions of employment may be required to ensure that the contract is retained in-house (this issue is explored later in the chapter).

The importance of the *compulsory* element in tendering can be understood if it is set in the context of the *voluntary* local authority initiatives in competitive tendering. These have been given a significant amount of publicity because of the activities of 'flagship' London councils such as Wandsworth and Westminster. This might give the impression that government legislation bringing in compulsion was simply following a trend which was already well established, at least in Conservative-controlled councils. However, initiatives of the Wandsworth type are the exception rather than the rule as far as voluntary moves to introduce CT are concerned. Thus, a *Local Government Chronicle* survey of activities contracted out to the private sector over the period 1981–7 found that their total value was only £75 million (Fretwell 1988: 4). In contrast, a recent Local Government Management Board survey covering 3,475 contracts in England and Wales under the *compulsory* tendering provisions of the Local Government Act 1988, found that the total value of these contracts was £1,825.4 million (Local Government Management Board 1992: 7).

The same survey provides a valuable source on the distribution of contract wins between DSOs and outside contractors. Table 4.2 shows that the majority of contracts so far have been won by DSOs and that this advantage is magnified when account is taken of contract values with DSOs tending to win the higher-value contracts.

**Table 4.2** DSO success rate in compulsory competitive tendering under the Local Government Act 1988 in England and Wales: rounds to January 1992

| Activity | DSO success % of contracts | DSO success % of value of contracts won by DSOs |
|---|---|---|
| Building cleaning | 57.8 | 84.9 |
| Refuse collection | 70.5 | 76.4 |
| Other cleaning | 73.0 | 82.1 |
| Vehicle Maintenance | 77.7 | 86.7 |
| Catering (education and welfare) | 93.6 | 97.5 |
| Catering (other) | 76.2 | 82.7 |
| Ground maintenance | 66.1 | 80.1 |
| Sports and leisure management | 76.6 | 74.7 |
| Average | 73.9 | 83.0 |

Source: Local Government Management Board (1992)

A similar pattern of in-house dominance operates in the NHS as is illustrated in Table 4.3.

**Table 4.3** Distribution of contracts wins between in-house suppliers and external contractors for support services in the NHS in the United Kingdom, 1989–90

| Activity | Contracts won (%) | |
| --- | --- | --- |
| | In-house | Contractor |
| Domestic | 80 | 20 |
| Catering | 96 | 4 |
| Laundry | 83 | 17 |
| Total | 86 | 14 |

Source Treasury (1991)

The differences in private and outsider contractor success rate is, in part, related to variation in the extent to which private contractors have demonstrated an interest in bidding in different areas. This is illustrated in the case of local government, in Table 4.4 where, again, figures are drawn from the 1992 Local Government Management Board survey (for similar findings drawn from an earlier sample of contracts, see Painter 1991: 203).

**Table 4.4** Number of contractors bidding and tendering for contracts by activity under the Local Government Act 1988 in England and Wales: Rounds to 1 January 1992

| Stage | Average number of contractors | | | |
| --- | --- | --- | --- | --- |
| | Building Cleaning | Refuse Collection | Vehicle Maintenance | Catering (Education and Welfare) |
| Applying | 19.0 | 13.0 | 11.6 | 6.3 |
| Tendering | 4.6 | 3.5 | 3.1 | 1.4 |

*Source*: Local Government Board (1992)

The pattern of relatively few bids in catering replicates the experience of the NHS. This illustrates a significant issue in CCT which was also taken up in chapter 3 on quasi-markets, that one of the difficulties posed by these structures involves the generation of adequate competition. That this is not forthcoming comes from the fact that private sector suppliers' objectives may flatly contradict the politically determined goals of government. Thus, for example,the catering contractor Gardner Merchant withdrew from two NHS contracts in 1984 when CCT was introduced. The grounds for this withdrawal were a preference for a form of contract where the contractor took a management fee but used NHS staff on their existing terms and conditions of employment (Sherman 1985: 806). However, this is in contradiction to government objectives to cut costs by driving down conditions of employment in such public sector services.

There is also marked regional variation in local government in the extent of DSO success. This is illustrated in the case of refuse collection in Table 4.5.

**Table 4.5** DSO success rate by region in refuse collection contracts in England and Wales under the Local Government Act 1988: rounds to 1 January 1992

| Region | DSO Success Rate % |
|---|---|
| Northern | 77.8 |
| Yorkshire & Humbershire | 95.0 |
| North West | 69.7 |
| East Midlands | 69.8 |
| West Midlands | 77.8 |
| East Anglia | 61.9 |
| South East | 61.1 |
| South West | 67.4 |
| Wales | 100 |
| London | 51.5 |

*Source*: Local Government Management Board (1992)

The Local Government Management Board survey does not directly show the relationship between DSO or contractor wins and the political control of the local authorities concerned. However, a *Local Government Chronicle* survey of contracts awarded in 1990 shows that, while DSOs win a higher share of contracts by value in Labour-controlled authorities, the contrast is not as sharp as might be anticipated. In Conservative-controlled authorities DSOs still won over three-quarters of the contracts by value; see Table 4.6.

**Table 4.6** Share of the total value of contracts won by DSOs under the Local Government Act 1988 by political control of authority: contracts awarded in 1990

| Controlling party | Value of DSO wins (millions) | Total Contract value (millions) | DSO share % |
|---|---|---|---|
| Labour | £714 | £813.6 | 87.7 |
| Conservative | £342.3 | £446.8 | 76.6 |

*Source*: Railings and Thrasher (1990)

It would, thus appear that political polarisation between Labour and Conservative over CCT, at least with respect to the decision whether to award the contract in-house or contract it out, is not a universal feature of British politics, but is mediated by regional determinants. Thus, Table 4.7, which is drawn from a survey of refuse collection and street cleaning contracts in London, shows a sharp divergence in practice quite distinct from the more marginal differences in the overall pattern shown in Table 4.6.

**Table 4.7** Refuse collection and street cleaning contracts in London by political control of authority: contracts awarded, 1989–91

| Political control of the authority | Awarded in-house | Awarded to contractor | In-house success rate % |
|---|---|---|---|
| Labour | 18 | 2 | 90 |
| Conservative | 6 | 12 | 33 |

*Source*: McGuirk (1991)

# CCT and 'Savings'

Central to arguments in favour of CCT have been the claimed links between the introduction of competition for the services covered and the savings that are said to accrue. In this respect, according to contestable market justifications for CCT, it is immaterial whether the contract is won in-house or not since the introduction of competition is seen as creating efficiency gains and thus lower costs. It will be necessary to examine the concept of efficiency later in the argument. However, in this section the aim will be to look at the evidence on 'savings'.

It is worth beginning by making the point that there is no necessary link between competition and lower costs. This is illustrated, in particular, by evidence from the United States on forms of service provision. This provides an interesting contrast because refuse collection services are provided in the United States in much more varied forms than are encountered in the United Kingdom. Not only are there in-house providers competing with outside contractors but, in certain areas, there are direct contracts between householders and private collection firms. The latter is, of course, not only a 'competitive' variant but also, in contrast to tendering, a 'consumerist' variant. A study of refuse collection by Stevens (1984) attempted to control for various features of service delivery such as frequency of collection and the point from which refuse is collected, features which are likely to influence collection costs. She found that 'competitive' arrangements (where householders contract directly with suppliers) were, varying with the size of the city, 26–48 per cent more costly than situations where a private contractor collected all the refuse in a given area. Two reasons were given for the increased cost of this type of provision. One was the fact that contracts were with *particular* customers; thus the collector would not have the franchise to collect from each household in the area and thus lose any scale economy advantages. The other has connections with issues raised in chapter 3, since it concerns the transaction costs associated with markets. Thus, Stevens was told by her management respondents that the costs of billing customers and collecting charges accounted for as much as 15 per cent of revenue (ibid.).

If, however, competitive processes *per se* do not guarantee savings because of the effects of technical problems and administrative costs this is not a criticism of CT. Thus, it could be argued that CT involves the 'disciplining' effects of competition without the cost drawbacks associated with direct contact between consumers and contractors.

The question of assessing cost savings raises tricky methodological problems. Broadly speaking two sorts of approach have been used: one attempts to use models to generate expected cost figures for a given pattern of service in a particular physical environment. Part of the rationale for this approach was indicated earlier in the discussion of the Stevens study. The costs of providing a service like refuse collection will be affected by features such as the point of collection (e.g. kerbside or backgarden) and the distance to the waste disposal dump. The model attempts to capture such differences in expected cost figures which vary with the service provision and environmental characteristics. Such an approach has been used to evaluate CT by looking at the relationship between actual and expected costs in local authorities and then examining whether there is a relationship to CT.

For example, a study by the Audit Commission, undertaken before the introduction of CCT, compared the relationship between actual and expected costs in authorities which had contracted out their refuse collection services with those where an in-house DLO provided the service. This study found that there were on average no cost differences between the best 25 per cent private and DLO operators (both averaged 4 per cent below the expected cost standard). However, *overall* private contractors operated with lower costs, for example the average costs in the worst 25 per cent of private contractors was equivalent to the expected cost figure while the average for the corresponding DLOs was 16 per cent above the expected cost standard (Audit Commission 1984: 20). In principle such methods have advantages since they aim to control for features of service provision and the context in which the service is provided. However, equally, this means that the reliability of the results depend on the specification of the model. If features which have a significant effect on costs are not captured, then the results will not be reliable.

An alternative approach is to compare service costs over time, before and after a tendering process. However, where this is done a crucial condition is that no significant change has been made in the specification of the service. For example, if the scope of a service is reduced (fewer collections, smaller area cleaned) then it is easier to perform, should require less labour, materials and equipment and thus can be completed more cheaply. Finally, some attempt should be made to assess service 'quality' since lower costs might be an effect of performing the service to a lower standard.

As far as comparisons over time are concerned, it is striking how often this condition is infringed. Thus Bach points out that a study by Milne (1987) claims savings within the NHS due to greater efficiency as an effect of CCT (Bach 1989: 4). However, the same study concluded that in three (out of six) contracts studied, 'a major reduction in total expenditure resulted from a change in specification' (Milne 1987: 153).

A similar failure to distinguish savings via lower costs for a given activity and re-specification of the activity occurs in a National Audit Office study of competitive tendering in the NHS. The study examined twenty-nine contracts in domestic, catering and laundry services in four Regions. Again, there were areas in which savings were claimed to have occurred. However, the same report points out that drawing up specifications 'cause authorities to undertake a thorough review of service requirements' (National Audit Office 1987: 18). As a consequence,' particularly in relation to domestic services the reviews indicated scope for rationalising existing operations e.g. by reductions in tasks and frequency of cleaning' (ibid.) (see also Treasury 1986: 25 for a similar case).

A further difficulty in defining savings relates to the effects of CT on other service providers. Thus, in the case of hospital cleaning it has been argued that the impact of CT is both to define the job more narrowly as an effect of contract specification and increase the demands of the cleaning task so that greater areas need to be cleaned in a given working period. As a consequence, tasks previously undertaken by domestic staff tend to be displaced on to nurses. Thus a formal cost saving could result in the transfer of activities to other staff not covered by the contract (Bach 1989: 16; Bragg 1988: 336).

Similar problems arise with respect to issues of service quality. Again, a peculiarity of many accounts is that savings are cited in abstraction from any discussion of the impact on service quality. Thus, a general review of the effects of competitive tendering argues that the evidence is 'supportive of the claim that large efficiency gains are possible in the provision of local services' (Parker and Hartley 1990: 14). Yet the same study goes on to argue that 'most of the relevant studies have focussed on costs of production though a number have endeavoured to control for changes in the quality of service' (ibid).

There are parallels in specific services. In the NHS an additional incentive to CT has been the introduction of Cost Improvement Improvement Programmes (CIPs). Under this system NHS managers are required to develop programmes to achieve a regular reduction in costs. These programmes have also taken on a political significance in that what are claimed as 'cumulative savings' from such programmes are included in the annual Public Expenditure White Papers.

A study by the King's Fund Institute of three District Health Authorities found that savings attributed to CT could loom large in CIPs. In 1987–8 one of the Districts studied claimed cost savings of £512,000 of which £215,000 were attributed to savings resulting from CT (King's Fund 1988: 21).

In principle, these should be genuine savings since the formal definition of CIPs issued by the then DHSS stressed that cuts in provision should not be included: 'cash releasing cost improvements are measures aimed at improving the use of resources by reducing the costs of running a service *while achieving the same, or higher levels of service output.*' (King's Fund 1988: 6; our emphasis).

The identification of CIPs should thus require a process of monitoring where savings could be distinguished from service reductions. Yet it has been a standard finding of investigations of CIPs that effective monitoring of these programmes is relatively rare. A National Audit Office study of 1986 found that 'the information supplied by Districts often appeared to be readily accepted by RHAs in contrast to the important review responsibility envisaged for regions...' (National Audit Office 1986: 9).

The King's Fund found similar difficulties in two Districts in their study, which claimed substantial gains from CT. In one case there were differences between local managers over whether a decline in standards had occurred, or indeed how 'quality' should be measured with respect to the services concerned (King's Fund 1988: 20). In another District 'savings' of £800,000 from CT had been claimed as part of the CIP programme in 1986–7, but subsequently managers interviewed in the District took the view that these contracts had been underpriced and had led to problems with maintaining acceptable standards (King's Fund 1988: 23).

Elsewhere in this book reference has been made to the difficulties involved in assessing service 'quality' in the public sector. Usually, these difficulties have been related to relatively complex services involving elements of professional judgement and a plurality of diverse perspectives from which the services might be judged. CCT does not appear to pose such problems. Thus, for example, two American commentators looking at the characteristics of services 'most frequently contracted by local government' in the United States claim that one of the defining features is that they have 'easily monitored outputs' (Chandler and Feuille 1991: 16).

However, while the problems are not as marked in the services which have been subject to CCT the contrast can be exaggerated. In their argument for easily measured 'outputs', Chandler and Feuille refer to purely quantitative features, such as numbers of meals served, yet this says nothing about the standard of service provided (ibid). These difficulties raise problems for claims of 'savings' and these can cut both ways.

Many critics of CCT have argued that the process is regularly accompanied by a decline in service standards. However, again there are difficulties in substantiating such claims. In Bach's case study of CT in a new District General Hospital a private contractor initially won the contract. However, following dissatisfaction with its performance the contract was returned 'in-house'. Given that service management at District level in this case were sympathetic to CT, the return in-house is unlikely to be related to any anti-contractor bias. Bach claims that low staffing levels and training standards contributed not only to poor standards but also to a sharp increase in the spread of infection. Bach argued that the link to infection was the spread of a micro-organism, Methicillin Resistant Staphyloccus Aureus (MRSA), which can affect patients via infected dust (Bach 1985: 12). The private contractor was cleaning the hospital over the period February 1985-September 1986. In 1985 nine patients were identified as MRSA positive and sixty in 1986, with the peak of infection levels in August 1986. As part of the contract cleaning standards were monitored and overall performance was expressed as 'satisfactory' inspections as a percentage of the total number of inspections (Bach 1989: 21). Bach goes on to argue that the most virulent effects of MRSA were felt when the performance level was at its lowest. Furthermore, when the contract was returned in-house cleaning performance improved and the number of MRSA cases fell.

However, there are a number of difficulties in Bach's account. It is not clear what criteria were applied to determine when cleaning was 'satisfactory'. Similarly, Bach admits that MRSA is not merely spread via infected dust but also directly from person to person (ibid.) and that, 'the difficulties with MRSA cannot be solely attributed to standards of cleaning as screening processes and nursing practices have an impact on the spread of MRSA' (ibid.).

The subjectivity of standards of quality in services subject to CT can also be illustrated from a US study which comes to diametrically opposed conclusions to that of Bach. A study by Stevens concluded *both* that there were major cost differences between public and private sector after adjusting for levels of service and that,'without exception, differences in service quality were not found to explain differences in service cost' (Stevens 1984: 399 and 401). However, many of the measures of 'quality' used were either highly subjective or reduced quality to simple quantitative measures of activity as Table 4.8 indicates.

**Table 4.8** Measures of 'level of service' in public services

| Service | Criteria for 'Level of Service' |
| --- | --- |
| Street sweeping | Sweepings/year |
| Refuse collection | Frequency and pick-up location |
| Payroll | % of checks to salaried employees |
| Traffic signal maintenance | No. preventive maintenance visits per intersection per year |

*Source*: Stevens (1984)

The whole question of savings thus remains an ambiguous one. It is common to find 'savings' when it is unclear whether the specification has been changed and definitions of service 'quality' remain elusive.

## The Impact on Labour

If the effects of CCT on service cost and quality has defined one of the areas of debate on competitive tendering the effects on labour has raised issues of an even more directly political form. This issue turns on both an empirical question and an issue involving political values. The empirical question is, if CCT results in cost reductions (this term is chosen to bracket the question of whether such reductions constitute 'savings'), how far are these reductions at the expense of the labour force? The question of political values relates to how the sources of such cost reductions should be viewed. However, before that question can be posed, it is necessary to look at the question of the source of cost reductions.

Some accounts are quite unequivocal on this issue, arguing that cost reductions are derived from the effect of CCT on conditions of employment. Furthermore, such accounts do *not* exclusively derive from trade-union sources where there may be an interest in stressing the negative effects on workers. For example, the report of a multi-departmental review on competitive tendering in central government, cited earlier, which was favourable to CT argued that 'Most of the savings from contracting out arise because contractors offer poorer conditions of employment...they eliminate costly bonus schemes and overtime working, provide little if any sick pay,and avoid national insurance payments by means of more part-time working' (Treasury 1986: 33). Equally, the report also stressed that contractor cost advantages were not an effect of technical superiority in methods used but rather the nature of the regime applied to direct labour: 'The evidence that contractors in the ancillary services are technically ahead of managers in the public sector is patchy. Where the contractors have the edge is in the toughness of their management' (Treasury 1986: 34).

Similar conclusions were reached by a survey of the effects of CT in the United States: 'a good deal of what taxpayers stand to gain from privatization comes at the expense of municipal employee' (Donahue 1989: 144–5).

In the British context there is evidence to support such contentions. Bach's case study provides valuable material on the cost structure and the sources of contractor cost reductions in hospital cleaning. In this particular service the role of direct labour in the total cost is striking. Bach found that, of the five bidders for the hospital cleaning contract (one in-house, four private contractors) labour costs accounted for over 90 per cent of total costs in all cases (Bach 1989: 7). In this particular exercise the contract was won first by a private contractor. Bach's study shows that the contract price quoted by the winning contractor (for a two-year contract) was nearly 30 per cent lower than the in-house bid. Examining the means by which the contractor could quote such a substantially lower bid Bach's finding are similar to the conclusions reached by the inter-departmental study of central government departments: the contractor's bid operated with staffing levels, in terms of Whole Time Equivalents, over 20 per cent below the level of the in-house bid (ibid.). This study also examined detailed costings, which showed the importance not just of total staffing levels but also the distribution of working hours. Thus, while there was little difference in basic pay rates between the in-house bid and the contractor, the latter reduced or eliminated bonus payments and substituted part-time for full-time labour. The effect of the latter was to bring a large percentage of staff below the national insurance threshold, thus eliminating the employer's national insurance contribution. A corollary of such a policy was, of course, to eliminate national insurance contributions but it equally meant that the employees concerned lost any cover from state contributory benefits.

A further indication of the impact on labour of CCT derives from survey evidence. In May 1990 the journal *Bargaining Report* published a survey of the impact on pay and conditions in 300 contracts covered by the requirements of the Local Government Act 1988. The overall pattern of contract wins was consistent with the findings of most surveys with the vast majority (89.6 per cent) of contracts won by the DSO. The biggest impact on conditions was found in employment levels. Table 4.9 shows the effects where contracts were won by DSOs that, overall, job cuts occurred in just over half of all contracts surveyed and in excess of 70 per cent of contracts in 'other cleaning' and refuse collection. Cuts in hours were somewhat less significant in general but occurred in over half of building cleaning and over 40 per cent of school/welfare catering contracts. Clearly, even where DSO wins were recorded this did not mean that the *status quo ante* with respect to labour was retained.

However, this is certainly not a universal view. A British study of costs in refuse collection contrasted costs in local authorities which had put the service out to tender where an in-house win occurred, tenders won by private contractors and authorities which had not put the service out to tender. The data were drawn from 1984 and thus preceded the introduction of *compulsory* competitive tendering. The study attempted to measure differences in 'technical efficiency' between the local authorities concerned. The method seeks to identify a minimum volume of labour and vehicles which will be required to produce the output (for example, 1 tonne of refuse). Service providers operating at this minimum level are defined as 'technically efficient'. Conversely, authorities with inputs in excess of this minimum level diverge from 'technical efficiency'. A simple example can be used to illustrate what would count as an example of 'technical inefficiency'. Assuming that two local authorities are providing a similar refuse-collection service (e.g. number of collections in a given period, similar levels of spillage, etc.) and in a similar set of circumstances (e.g. proximity to the dump); and that both are using identical capital equipment, authority A is operating at the frontier of technical efficiency with the minimum input of labour required, in contrast, authority B is using more labour than A and thus diverges from the norm of technical efficiency. It is equally possible to quantify the gap between the authorities. Cubbin el al. use this methodology to examine the effects of CT, and the results are reported in Table 4.10.

**Table 4.9** The Impact of CCT on conditions of employment: contracts awarded 1989–90 and won by the DSO; percentage of contracts affected by the changes concerned

|  | Job cuts | Pay cuts | Bonus pay Cuts | Hours cuts | Holiday Cuts |
|---|---|---|---|---|---|
| School/ Welfare Catering | 28.5 | 14.2 | – | 42.8 | 14.2 |
| Other Catering | 31.5 | 10.5 | – | 15.7 | 5.2 |
| Ground maintenance | 40.7 | 5.2 | 6.5 | 5.2 | 3.9 |
| Vehicle maintenance | 44.0 | – | 4.0 | – | – |
| Building cleaning | 8.9 | 25.6 | 15.3 | 51.2 | 17.9 |
| Other cleaning | 72.7 | 9.0 | 4.5 | 4.5 | 4.5 |
| Refuse collection | 70.9 | 6.4 | – | – | 16.1 |
| Total | 50.9 | 10.0 | 5.9 | 16.7 | 8.5 |

Source: *Bargaining Report* (1990)

**Table 4.10** 'Efficiency' comparisons: refuse collection; local authorities in England and Wales, 1984–5

|  | 'Technical<br><br>Mean | Efficiency'<br><br>'Efficiency'<br>differences | Regression<br>based<br>cost<br>differences |
|---|---|---|---|
| 1. All authorites | (317) 0.8142 | – | – |
| 2. Tendered and<br>   contracted out | ( 17) 0.9390 (2 and 3) | 17% | 22% |
| 3. Not tendered | (291) 0.8055 |  |  |
| 4. Tendered and<br>   retained in-house | (9) 0.8608 (2 and 4) | 7% | 17% |

*Source*: Cubbin et al. (1987)

Technical efficiency is represented here by a score of 1 and thus the nearer authorities were to 1 the more technically efficient they were. Equally, the technical-efficiency gap would be defined by the ratio of mean scores. Thus, in the table the 17 per cent efficiency difference is simply derived by expressing the technical-efficiency scores of the tendering and contracting-out authorities with that for the 'not tendered' authorities.

It is important to bear in mind that the technical-efficiency comparisons are contrasting variations in inputs in *physical,* not cost, terms. Thus, in the example used above the efficiency standard is not defined by reference to the cost of labour (wages, non-wage benefits etc.), but rather the volume of labour measured in labour hours. The next stage in the argument is to relate this 'physical efficiency' measure to an overall measure of *cost* differences between the sets of authorities covered. The cost difference figures are, in fact, drawn from a previous study. As can be seen from the table most of the cost difference between tendered and contracted-out authorities and not-tendered authorities (22%) is 'explained' by the difference in 'technical efficiency'. Cubbin et al. draw the following conclusion from this study: 'Some commentators have asserted that the savings are largely the result of pecuniary losses of those in employment through lower wages and fringe benefits. Our results do not support that view. They indicate that for those authorities with private contractors the bulk of the savings can be attributed to improvements in technical efficiency – that is, physical productivity of both men and vehicles' (Cubbin et al. 1987: 53–4).

Some American commentators have also concluded that savings from tendering are derived from efficiency gains which are not at the expense of labour. The Stevens study of eight activities supplied by municipal services and outside contractors, cited average wage levels for contractors of $1,521 for private contractors and $1,442 for municipal providers.

Part of the reason for the difference in these conclusions relates to the aspects of the impact on the workforce considered. Thus, for example, Cubbin et al. are simply concerned with the issue of pay and fringe benefits. Furthermore, in so far as lower cost levels are related to lower staffing levels (a condition of technical efficiency) the argument is clearly compatible with the survey evidence on refuse cleaning cited earlier where pay cuts *per se* were relatively infrequent (see Table 4.9).

A further reason for discrepancies relates to the use of measures which are misleading. For example, the Stevens comparison of salary figures is an *unweighted* average figure. The significance of this fact can be seen from Table 4.11.

**Table 4.11** Labour cost and privatisation in eight municipal services in the United States

| Service | Average labour cost for the service as a share of city budget % | Municipal wages for the service relative to contractor wage % |
|---|---|---|
| Refuse collection | 1.89 | 115 |
| Turf maintenance | 1.40 | 129 |
| Tree maintenance | 0.91 | 106 |
| Traffic Signal maintenance | 0.46 | 115 |
| Street cleaning | 0.41 | 103 |
| Janitorial services | 0.33 | 140 |
| Asphalt laying | 0.26 | 63 |

*Source*: Donahue (1989)

This shows that in only one service area, asphalt laying, were municipal wage levels lower than those paid by contractors. Equally, the gains to labour in this case are less significant because this is the most capital-intensive of the processes of the services studied (Donahue 1989: 143).

The significance of labour cost differences in the more labour-intensive activities are illustrated in Donahue's analysis of Stevens' figures on grass-cutting. Stevens found that municipal costs for mowing an acre of grass averaged $81 as against $58 for contractors. However, if contractors had been obliged to offer the same wage levels as municipal contractors their costs would have risen to $73 an acre (Donahue 1989: 144).

These differences are related in part to the range of issues examined and the measures deployed. However, there is also an important question of wider significance raised by studies such as that of Cubbin et al. In assessing the impact on at least those workers who remain in employment, this article concentrates simply on the pay ('pecuniary') aspect. Yet this is a peculiarly narrow approach, since it abstracts completely from the nature of the employment regime under which workers do their job.

In this respect it is instructive to return to this article and look at what Cubbin et al. argue concerning the nature of the efficiency improvements, which they claim to have identified. In particular, two features are stressed: it is argued that 'task and finish' payment schemes, where employees are expected to finish a particular 'task' rather than work a given fixed number of hours, have become a 'major impediment to better productivity' (Cubbin et al. 1987.: 54). The basis for this argument is that such schemes can result in an increasing divergence between the original conditions assumed in the time set to complete a round and the conditions currently prevailing: 'The workload associated with a given "round" often diminishes with the passage of time following changes in routes and reductions in the number of units served. However, as payment levels remain the same, this has the effect of raising labour costs over and above the minimum required to collect a fixed volume of refuse' (Cubbin et al. 1987: 54).

The second factor which is claimed to be the source of 'efficiency' gains is the ability to vary crew size and rostering practices so that the deployment of crews and vehicles can be' closely matched to the pattern of demand' (ibid.).

There are a number of points which should be noted in this argument. In themselves the factors to which the study refers are speculative. Thus, they are not based on any attempt by the authors to investigate the actual working practices involved. However, what is striking is how far they refer to a deterioration in the conditions of employment. Thus, in the case of 'task and finish', what is assumed is that contractors will 'tighten up' and expect a given job to be completed in a shorter time. Note, incidentally, the ingenuous treatment of the bonus scheme here. The deliberations of work-study engineers here take on a scientific and normative character. Thus a *de facto* loosening of conditions of labour here is treated as a move away from the norm. This fails to appreciate the contentious character of work study and its inevitably subjective character.

The second feature emphasised also involves a deterioration in the conditions of labour; 'closely matching' labour requirements to levels of demand must involve a greater level of effort and less non-working time for the reduced labour force.

Thus, in their reductionist treatment of the impact on labour Cubbin et al. unconsciously reproduce the Hayekian assumption that the labour of the employee, once the contract has been struck, is and should be at the total discretion of the employer. Such a situation is not a loss to labour. There is another crucial point here. The technical frontier concept used by Cubbin et al. suggests that such changes in the labour regime constitute an advance in 'technical efficiency'. Indeed, this is quite consistent with the concept itself since a reduction in employment levels with a given level of output maintained represents such an 'efficiency' advance. Yet there is a paradoxical aspect to such a conceptual treatment. The claim that an efficiency advance has been achieved is derived from the idea that a given output has been achieved with fewer inputs. Yet these inputs are defined purely in terms of measures such as labour *hours,* abstracting from what happens in such hours. Yet central to such an argument is, to use a term cited earlier, the role of 'tough' management in coercing labour to increase its input.

It is also worth noting that such abridgements to the freedoms of workers at the workplace are a characteristic of the contracting-out and tendering process in the United States. Thus, Table 4.12 shows some systematic differences between municipal agencies and private contractors as employers.

**Table 4.12** Differences between employment practices between municipal agencies and contractors in a sample of cities in the United States

|  | Cities using contractors | Cities using municipal agencies |
| --- | --- | --- |
| Workforce unionised | 20.0% | 48.1% |
| Average age of workers | 32.1 years | 36.1 years |
| Vacation days per worker | 10.1 | 14.0 |
| Foremen with power to dismiss workers | 53.7% | 16.0% |
| Written reprimands used | 33.8% | 72.5% |
| Formal staff meetings held | 53.8% | 81.5% |

*Source*: Stevens (1984)

This raises the issue of political values. It is by no means clear that improvements in standards of service and cost reductions in public sector activities involve deteriorations in the conditions of labour. However, it is obvious that cost reductions (whether 'savings' or not) have been derived from enforcing a deterioration conditions for employees.

It is equally important to bear in mind that this issue is often not confronted directly. In many discussions of CT the whole issue is reduced to one of whether tendering is associated with lower costs at a given level of service. Indeed, this is the dominant standpoint adopted in contemporary *economic* analysis of CCT. In these analyses the producers of the service and their interests have virtually vanished from view.

A good illustration of this type of argument is provided by a debate on the sources of CT cost reductions between Ganley and Grahl (1988) on one side and Domberger et al. (1988) on the other.

Ganley and Grahl make a number of points similar to those made above with respects to the cost to labour involved in CCT: that changes in working practices under CT and CCT have been made under implicit or explicit threats of redundancy; that the costs to labour cannot be reflected simply in financial costs.

In response to these contentions Domberger et al. produce a rather confused argument. On one hand, they seek to refute Ganley and Grahl's argument that CT cost reductions are not made at the expense of the labour force. The argument is somewhat puzzling since they admit that CCT will involve 'some redistribution of benefits from producers to consumers' (Domberger et al. 1988: 88)

This implicit view that labour does lose as a result of CCT is reinforced later, when Domberger et al. attack Ganley and Grahl's argument on normative grounds: 'it seems likely that public sector monopoly provision enabled monopoly rents to be expropriated by the work force' and 'if it turns out that the best case that can be made for the retention of a public sector monopoly in refuse collection is that it provides the basis for expropriation of monopoly rents,then this seems to us to be compelling argument *in favour* of the introduction rather than the reverse' (Domberger et al. 1988: 89; emphasis in the original).

However, this appears to lead to a rather extraordinary conclusion. The workers affected by the operation of CCT are, predominantly, unskilled and semi-skilled and thus relatively poorly paid. For example, a survey of contract cleaners in 1990 found that over half were paid around £2 per hour or less (Bargaining Report 1990: 12). It also found that unionised cleaners were paid significantly higher rates. This is the kind of 'rent' which, according to this argument, ought to be removed. It is true that the protections accorded by the absence of contestable markets will not help the group still subject to the effects of competition. Quite reasonably it might then be argued that, if the aim is to protect all such low-paid employees, then this calls for regulation rather than public sector monopoly. However, this abstracts from the fact that the experience of labour market regulation is that legal rights do not tend to be effective in the absence of collective bargaining (Brown 1991: 219). It is, thus, difficult to reconcile at least cost-saving oriented CCT, with employment protection via a regulatory framework since the process tends to involve de-unionisation as was demonstrated earlier.

To return to the theme with which the chapter started, it seems clear that any evaluation of CCT cannot avoid political questions. These are twofold: as labour tends to be the loser there is a political question concerning the distributional effects issues that take us back to the debates on the New Right. And there is a related question: in Chapter One (Table 1.3 pp.22–3) it was demonstrated that the Conservative election victories of the 1980s were achieved with a relatively modest share of the vote; in the last three elections, they have achieved a share of the vote lower than that attained when they *lost* in 1964. The second political question which this raises is, does this give central government a warrant to impose a policy of CCT on local authorities and regions where the anti-producer-group values which underlie it have been rejected?

# 5

## Determining Public Sector Pay: Prescription and Practice

In this chapter we shall consider the approach taken by successive Conservative governments to the determination of pay in the public sector. With public sector pay representing roughly 60 per cent of current spending on goods and services (Bailey and Trinder 1989: 1), pay settlements in the sector have a major impact on total public spending. A concern with the latter became an issue of ideological significance for the Conservatives. With the shift to the right in the British Conservative Party in the 1970s, discussed in chapter 1, the public sector became increasingly seen in negative terms. For example, criticising what he saw as the effects of public spending in the era of the 'middle way', Keith Joseph argued: 'The public sector, including central and local government, and more accurately named the state-sector or wealth-eating sector...spread like bindweed at the expense of the non-state sector, the wealth-creating sector, strangling and threatening to destroy what it grew upon' (cited in Eccleshall 1990: 236). This was in line with a view which had become increasingly fashionable among academics and journalists. A much quoted work was that of Robert Bacon and Walter Eltis, *Britain's Economic Problem: Too Few Producers*. These authors argued that the growth of the non-marketed sector of the economy drew resources (both financial and personnel) away from the marketed sector, that is the production of goods and services for sale. Yet it was the latter that was responsible for the creation of wealth. By the 1970s, a declining marketed sector was supporting a bloated non-marketed sector. It took only a small step to identify the latter as the cause of Britain's economic decline, a view clearly expressed in the Conservative Party's first White Paper on public spending when they came into office in 1979: 'Public expenditure is at the heart of Britain's economic difficulties. Over the years public spending has been increased on assumptions about economic growth which have not been achieved. If this continued our economy would be threatened with endemic inflation and economic decline' (Treasury 1979: 1).

Thus the *economic* desirabilty of shrinking the public sector was established as a central tenet of the philosophy of that and subsequent Conservative governments of the 1980s. A policy of reducing public expenditure has implications for employment in the public sector: a really radical reduction in public spending would involve sharply cutting the number of public sector employees and at first sight the figures on public sector employment seem to indicate that successive Conservative governments did pursue such a radical approach. The estimated workforce in employment in 1980 was 25.3 million of which 17.9 million (71 per cent) were employed in the private sector, the remainder, 7.3 million (29 per cent), in the public sector (Central Statistical Office 1991: 98).

By mid-1991, the public sector share of the total workforce had declined to 5.9 million (22.4 per cent) (ibid.: 98). However, this was predominantly the effect of the privatisation programme which switched nationalised industries into the private sector. This can be seen in Table 5.1, which examines the pattern of public sector employment in the public sector in 1979, when the Conservatives came into office and in 1991.

**Table 5.1** Public Sector Employment in the United Kingdom 1979 and 1991 (000s)

|      | NHS   | Total central government | Total local government | Nationalised industries sector | Total public |
|------|-------|--------------------------|------------------------|--------------------------------|--------------|
| 1979 | 1,152 | 2,387                    | 2,997                  | 1,849                          | 7,449        |
| 1991 | 1,092 | 2,177                    | 2,948                  | 516                            | 5,872        |

*Source*: CSO (1991: Table D )

Of the total fall in public sector employment of 1,577,000 between 1979 and 1991, 1,333,000, or 84 per cent, were accounted for by the privatisation programme. In contrast, employment in the major welfare service areas was relatively stable: social services employment increased and the fall in employment in education was under ten per cent over the period. Furthermore, the NHS figure for 1991 does not include 124,000 employees in NHS Trusts. If this figure is added into the NHS total, then overall NHS employment over the period increased.

Thus, if reluctantly, Conservative governments in the 1980s continued to remain substantial direct employers of labour and also responsible for funding a significant proportion of employment in the public sector as a whole. In this chapter we shall examine how they discharged this role of paymaster to the public sector. The chapter is divided into three sections. The first will explore the Conservative philosophy on pay and employment, contrasting this with the pattern of pay determination which was *in situ* in 1979; the challenges to this inheritance will be the focus of the second section; in both these sections it will be argued that the Conservatives operated with a norm which stressed the desirability of more individualised forms of pay determination. The third section will consider in detail one of the clearest manifestations of this approach, namely performance-related pay. The chapter ends with an a discussion of the overall effects of Conservative policy on public sector pay.

The Megaw Inquiry into Civil Service Pay (1982), the Review Bodies on Doctors' and Dentists' Remuneration, the Review Bodies for Nursing Staff, Midwives and Health Visitors and the Interim Advisory Committee on School Teachers' Pay and Conditions (1988–91), which was succeeded by the School Teachers' Review Body in 1992, provided forums where government could express their idea on pay determination. The reports of these bodies have, therefore, been used as exemplary texts throughout the chapter.

## Conservative philosophy on pay and employment

In the argument developed so far it has been pointed out that pay determination in the public sector was relevant for the Conservatives in terms of the economic goal of controlling public expenditure. It was also significant for broader ideological reasons. As we saw in chapter 1, concomitant with the rejection of Keynesian political economy was an alternative diagnosis of unemployment where changes in the supply side and in particular the labour market were viewed as crucial if unemployment was to be reduced and inflation controlled. Such objectives were themselves congruent with the political philosophy embodied, particularly in legislation on labour law, which was virulently anti-collectivist.

The implications of these ideological concerns for employment policy can be seen in two White Papers, 'Employment: Challenge for the Nation' (Department of Employment 1985) and 'Employment for the 1990s' (Employment Department 1988), which provide a clear statement of Conservative philosophy in the areas of pay and employment.

Eschewing the Keynesian approach to employment and unemployment, the 1985 White Paper states that the role of government in maintaining full employment is 'inescapably limited' to developing a frame-work of economic and industrial policy, removing obstacles to the creation of jobs and tackling the unemployment problems of groups with special needs (Department of Employment 1985: para. 4.2). For the Conservatives, 'the biggest single cause of high unemployment is the failure of our jobs market, the weak link in our economy'; 'the supply side is crucial, and that needs an efficient labour market' (ibid.: paras. 5.2 and 5.4). It is the responsibility of management, employees and the education system 'to ensure that the supply of labour meets demand in quality, quantity, cost and flexibility' (ibid.).

These themes are developed in the subsequent White Paper, where the barriers to employment are identified as industrial relations, pay and training. Trade union activity in the 1970s, it is argued, adversely affected labour costs, productivity and jobs; in short, such activity was synonymous with creating unemployment. For the future unions must accept that the job prospects of their members will be improved only 'by linking pay to the performance of the businesses for which they work and to local labour market conditions' (Employment Department 1988: para. 2.12).

Unlike the earlier White Paper, which says little on pay beyond reiterating familiar government themes of the 1980s, such as government-imposed pay policies do not work and hence pay bargaining is a matter solely for employers and employees, the institutions and the criteria by which pay is determined are a central feature of the 1988 White Paper. Following the by now expected genuflections to 'excessive pay increases', 'pay settlements remaining too high', comes a key statement of the changes required in pay bargaining if future employment growth is to be secured. 'Many existing approaches to pay bargaining, beloved of trade unions and employers alike, will need to change if we are to secure the flexibility essential to employment' (Employment Department 1988: para. 3.5). Thus the 'going rate', 'comparability' and 'cost of living increases' are attacked as 'outmoded concepts' (ibid: para. 3.5). There were also criticisms of practice on both the timing of settlements and the level of bargaining; the assumption that pay should automatically rise annually was attacked; national pay bargaining being seen as engendering rigidities in the labour market.

Comparability was objectionable from two distinct points of view. It suggested that at least an element in pay determination should be a concern with equity. However, this raised the spectre of 'social justice' considerations entering into questions of pay determination. The rejection of such a position was an aspect of the Hayekian programme which had been embraced by the Conservatives, as instanced by the opposition to incomes policy and minimum wage legislation. In addition, comparability principles linked pay to the type of job performed, not to any measure of *performance* in the job. This was seen as inflationary in that it encouraged a divorce between pay increases and productivity improvements. This was also the basis for opposition to the concept of a 'rate for the job'. 'Paying the rate for the job' assumes that all workers will be treated in a uniform way and thus militates against rewarding individual performance and productivity. The extension of this form of argument also had implications for what was seen as the appropriate *level* at which bargaining should take place.

The White Paper put forward a particularly critical view of national pay bargaining. It argued that such agreements were a source of rigidity in that they prevented employers from adjusting wages to take account of different circumstances. It was further assumed that national agreements tended to inflate wages by constraining employers from reducing pay in areas of high unemployment and thus restricted the creation of job opportunities in such 'labour markets'. The preferred alternative would be decentralisation of pay bargaining (defined in geographical terms).

Underlying these arguments was a set of principles defining how pay determination should ideally operate. Of central importance here was the conception of an *individualised* employment relationship. As was indicated in chapter 1, this approach was central to Conservative legislation on individual and collective labour law: reducing the scope of individual employment rights removed state protection from the employee and legislation on the trade unions narrowed the range of collective action via mechanisms such as 'enterprise confinement'.

The attack on what were seen as prevailing patterns of wage determination was of a piece with such a stance. This was most clearly articulated in the conception of linking pay with 'performance' since here it was possible to move in the direction of distinct individual pay rates. The other arguments point in the same direction. Thus decentralised bargaining is again a potential force for differentiation; the link to political anti-collectivism is clear.

The general approach to pay determination favoured by the Conservatives thus suggested a number of objectives: an attack on collectivist *institutions* of pay determination; an attack on *criteria* of pay determination which involved concerns of social justice or other impediments to 'flexible' and differentiated 'adjustments' of the labour market.

In the private sector Conservative attempts to advance such an approach were necessarily limited. After all, pay determination was to be a matter of negotiation between employers and employees.

Government could exhort private employers to follow the prescribed road but that was as far as they could go. In contrast, in the public sector the government either was the direct employer or, where it was not, could exercise a crucial influence on pay determination. This was particularly significant given the *absence* of major privatisations of social services. In the rest of this chapter the aim is to examine how the government used its power as paymaster. However, if one is to set this in context, it is necessary to look at the pattern of pay determination in the public sector when the Conservatives came into office in 1979.

## Public Sector Pay Determination: 1979

### Institutions

The 1979 Conservative government inherited a number of different arrangements for determining pay in the public sector: collective bargaining, review bodies, indexation and *ad hoc* pay inquiries. The majority of public sector employees had their pay determined by national collective bargaining, either the Burnham or Whitley systems. The former, for teachers, dated from 1945 and was a tripartite structure with representatives of local authorities, central government and the unions. The role of the Minister of Education was to approve the settlements agreed by the employers and unions, which then had statutory force. The balance of power in this structure changed somewhat with the Remuneration of Teachers Act 1965. Under this Act central government secured a veto over the global sums available for teacher's pay and a weighted vote over the distribution of any award (Saran and Sheldrake 1988 : 13). The Act also introduced the principle of unilateral arbitration in the case of disputes.

The Whitley system originated in 1916 as a mechanism for improving employer-employee relationships in the engineering industry: it was extended to local authorities and the public utilities in 1918, and by 1979 covered civil servants, local authority employees, other than the police and teachers, and NHS employees, with the exception of doctors and dentists (Bailey and Trinder 1989: 16). Although the structure of Whitley varies for the different groups, Bailey and Trinder have argued that Whitleyism itself is characterised by a number of principles: joint agreement between employers and employees on pay and conditions; negotiations between those two parties; collective bargaining within an agreed framework; procedures for conciliation or arbitration (ibid.: 16–17).

Review bodies are appointed by the government but are independent of it. They make recommendations on the size of the pay increase for particular occupational groups: the government is then free to accept or reject the recommendations or delay payment by staging the awards. The review bodies for the armed forces, doctors and dentists, and senior civil servants, senior officers of the armed forces and the judiciary were established in 1971 under the Heath government.

A pay formula was introduced for the police in 1978. This linked the rise in pay to the rate of increase in the average earnings index.

Finally, in the 1970s, governments resorted to *ad hoc* pay inquiries for specific groups of employees: for example, the Houghton Report on non-university teachers, 1974; the Halsbury Report on nurses also in 1974; the Edmund Davies Report on police, 1978; and the Clegg Commission on Pay Comparability, 1979–81. These inquiries usually followed pay freezes or incomes policies and were attempts to circumvent industrial action.

## Criteria

Until 1981, a key principle for determining pay in the public sector was that of 'fair comparison'. The seminal statement of this principle was that of the Priestley Inquiry into Civil Service Pay in 1955. Priestley was critical of its predecessor, the Tomlin Committee (1929–31) which had argued that the basis of remuneration for civil servants should be what was necessary to recruit and retain them without loss of keeness and efficiency (Priestley 1955: para. 87). Priestly rejected this 'law of the market' as an appropriate mechanism for determining civil-service pay (ibid.: para. 94). 'We believe that the State is under a categorical obligation to remunerate its employees fairly, and that any statement which does not explicitly recognise this is inadequate' (ibid: para. 90).

The Inquiry argued that rates of pay which allowed recruitment and retention of efficient staff were not necessarily fair and that any analysis of fairness solely in these terms could not be supported by the facts: first, financial considerations were not a principal incentive in attracting recruits to the civil service; second, low rates of turnover were not reliable indicators of the fairness or otherwise of pay; third, it could not be assumed that civil servants were fairly paid if they were carrying out their duties 'efficiently' (ibid.: paras 91–3). Thus Priestley recommended that the primary principle for determining civil service pay should be 'Fair comparison with the current remuneration of outside staffs employed on comparable work,taking account of differences in other conditions of service (ibid.: para. 177) Internal relativities could be used to supplement this primary principle.

Priestley also outlined a methodology for determining civil service pay in the future: namely the establishment of a Pay Research Unit which would have the task of comparing individual jobs inside and outside the civil service and reporting (to the government and civil service unions) on the actual rates of pay and all other relevant conditions of employment for the comparable jobs outside the civil service. This information would be the basis for the annual pay negotiations. (A fuller discussion of the pay research system can be found in chapters 2 and 3of the Megaw Inquiry of 1982). Priestley's recommendations were put into effect by the government and the pay research system, albeit with some modifications, continued until 1981.

Fair comparison became a significant influence in determining the pay of many other groups of public sector employees, not only civil servants from the 1950s onwards. However, the concept experienced a number of challenges. For example, the National Board for Prices and Incomes (NBPI), created in 1965 with the objective of stimulating efficiency in British industry, argued that comparability was incompatible with such an objective which required pay to be linked with productivity (Thomson and Beaumont 1978: 55). Incomes policies, for example, that of the Labour government in 1965 and the Social Contract of 1975, either downgraded or formally suspended all official comparabililty schemes. However, neither the NPBI nor incomes policies succeeded in eliminating the importance of fair comparison. Thus by 1969, the Board accepted that there was little alternative to its use in setting the pay of many public servants (Brown and Rowthorn 1990: 9). Similarly the Labour government in its Social Contract of 1975 rejected comparability, but in 1978 accepted the result of an inquiry into police pay which recommended that it be indexed to average national earnings (Bailey and Trinder 1989: 31–2). Following the 'Winter of Discontent' of 1979, the then Labour Government

> expressed a readiness to see a greater role for measuring pay and conditions (in public services) by making comparisons with pay and effort in other occupation. Government has a responsibility both to be fair to public service employees and to avoid arrangements which could in themselves prove inflationary. Comparability studies must therefore be made in a systematic and thorough manner (Hansard, vol. 963, col. 1252).

To undertake this work, a Standing Commission on Pay Comparability (Clegg) was established. Clegg produced ten reports in all covering teachers, nurses and midwives, NHS ancillary staff, among others. While not denying the relevance of labour supply and efficiency, Clegg was committed to the notion of 'fair comparison' as demonstrated by its method of working which attempted to use job-for-job comparisons. In all cases, Clegg recommended substantial increases in pay e.g. 16.9 per cent for local authority and NHS ancillaries, the equivalent of 18.2 per cent of the wage bill for teachers, in order to restore their wage levels to groups undertaking comparable work.

Thus public sector pay determination in 1979 was characterised by a mixture of collective bargaining, especially at national level, indexation and the influence of third-party recommendations, namely, review bodies, and with comparability as a key principle. As already argued, such institutions and principles did not correspond with Conservative economic ideology in the 1980s.

## Challenging the Inheritance

*Changing the Philosophy: Comparability*

The Conservative opposition had agreed to honour the findings of the Clegg Commission if there was a change of government following the 1979 election. The Conservative government did indeed honour the reports which appeared after its return to office in 1979, but then abolished the Commission in 1981.

The events surrounding the 1981 civil service pay negotiations were the catalyst for a further attack on fair comparison. In August 1980, the Government informed the unions that economic circumstances required tight constraint on public expenditure and this would influence the 1981 pay settlement. No agreed settlement was forthcoming over the following months. Thus, in October, the government withdrew from the pay agreements and pay research procedures for the 1981 settlement. Subsequent attempts to reach a settlement based on cash limits were unsuccessful and the civil service unions took selective industrial action from March to July 1981, when a settlement was reached. This period of industrial activity was accompanied by the appointment of the Megaw Inquiry into civil service pay in June 1981.

Megaw was critical of the 'fair comparison' principle espoused by Priestley. It argued that the pay research system introduced after Priestley was flawed in practice, pointing to such defects as the difficulties of finding comparator jobs in the private sector, the inflexibility and generosity of a formula which linked civil service pay to the median rate of pay of 'good employers' in the private sector, the undervaluation of index-linked pensions of civil servants and their relative job security. In addition, Megaw maintained that adherence to Priestley's primary principle of 'fair comparison' underestimated the importance of other factors such as internal relativities, recruitment and retention, financial and economic constraints, and management needs (Megaw Inquiry 1982: paras 80–4).

Taking account of both the adverse criticisms of the pay research system and the changed economic circumstances of the preceding years, namely, high levels of inflation and unemployment, Megaw recommended that in future, the governing principle for civil servants' pay should be what was necessary 'to recruit, retain and motivate them to perform efficiently the duties required of them at an appropriate level of competence' (ibid.: para. 91). In addition, internal relativities should play a more significant role than under the Priestley system (ibid.: ch.8).

The government pursued its attack on comparability by consistently urging the annual review bodies both for nursing staff and midwives (established in 1983, see below p. 117) and for doctors and dentists to reject it as a principle of pay determination. A few quotations will suffice:

> The Health Departments repeated their belief that the pay of nursing staff should not be governed primarily by comparisons with the pay of staff in other employments, still less with their own at some date. (Review Body for Nursing Staff, Midwives and Health Visitors 1987: para. 67).
>
> Direct comparability with other groups should not be the basis for determining the pay of public sector employees. Pay should be set rather at the appropriate level to ensure that sufficient employees of the right standard could be recruited and retained. (Review Body for Nursing Staff, Midwives and Health Visitors 1988: para. 63).
>
> Data about pay settlements and earnings movements should inform pay determination only to the extent that they were relevant to recruitment and retention. (Review Board for Nursing Staff, Midwives and Health Visitors 1991: para. 40)
>
> That when considering pay levels the main determinant should be what was sufficient to recruit, retain and motivate staff of the right quality and in the right numbers within the limits of affordability. (Review Body on Doctors' and Dentists' Remuneration 1991: para. 18).

The government also favoured market forces in setting teachers' pay in the period after the abolition of Burnham in 1987. Each of the remits provided by the Secretary of State for Education for Burnham's successor, the Interim Advisory Committee on School Teachers' Pay and Conditions, directed the Committee to have regard to 'The Government's view that school teachers' pay and conditions of service should be such as to enable the maintained school system to recruit, retain and motivate sufficient teachers of the required quality both nationally and at local level' (Interim Advisory Committee 1991: 7).

## Decentralisation

The antagonism of Conservative governments to national pay bargaining has already been documented: their preferred alternative was for the decentralisation of pay, which in turn embodied two distinct ideas; (1) the delegation of decisions on pay to the unit of employment e.g. school or hospital; (2) the introduction of regional variations in pay. The former is usually linked to problems of recruitment and retention of staff in a competitive labour market, and encompasses the possibility of pay rates which are *higher* than those nationally agreed. The latter also viewed nationally agreed pay rates as a constraint assuming that they were usually based on the 'going rate' in London and the South-East, and as such were assumed to contribute to high unemployment in areas of the country where the supply of labour exceeds the demand for it. Thus the objective of regional pay is to *reduce* overall pay levels.

In the Megaw Inquiry, the government (or rather individual departments) rehearsed their arguments on decentralisation and regional pay. Evidence put to the Inquiry questioned 'whether the rigidities which arise from centralism [of pay bargaining] are justified' (Megaw Inquiry 1982: para. 27). A major proponent for a measure of decentralisation was the Ministry of Defence: it argued that greater flexibility in pay would allow it to be more responsive to management needs, i.e. able to pay certain staff more than the nationally agreed rates. Both the Department of Health and Social Security and the Department of the Environment also favoured giving departments more discretion 'to vary pay in response to management requirements and market forces, particularly in respect of specialists' (ibid.: para. 280).

In its initial evidence to the Inquiry, the government asked it to consider regional pay variations. Megaw states the main arguments for this policy as follows: the civil service is probably paying more than it needs to in some areas to recruit and retain staff, and might be forcing up other employers' pay rates unnecessarily; conversely, the civil service may be paying too little in other areas and thus departments experience recruitment and selection difficulties; if a new pay system were to include comparisons with outside rates, these should reflect geographical differences where these are significant.

Support for decentralised pay can also be found in the Health Department's evidence to the Review Body for Nursing Staff, Midwives and Health Visitors in 1988 and 1990. In its evidence to the 1988

Review Body, the Health Departments supported some differentiation in the pay of nursing staff and suggested that there should be a pattern of general supplements to respond to recruitment and retention difficulties in London and discretionary supplements to be applied to other parts of the country. (Review Body for Nursing Staff, Midwives and Health Visitors 1988: para. 121). Whereas this proposal could be seen as a means of solving the London problem (that for discretionary payments was subsequently dropped), by the following year, the Health Departments had gone further stating that 'they were anxious to introduce more flexible remuneration arrangements which would enable pay levels to reflect differences in labour markets; and that they were particularly keen to see greater scope for geographical pay' (Review Body for Nursing Staff, Midwives and Health Visitors 1989: para. 110). They requested £5 million for 1989–90 for a pilot scheme to supplement national rates of pay for nurses and midwives selectively, again for recruitment and retention purposes. By 1990, selective pay had been transformed into flexible pay with Health Departments giving their objective as the introduction of 'comprehensive and systematic flexible pay arrangement within the NHS which would include a substantial element of local management discretion within a framework of minimum essential central control' (Review Body for Nursing Staff, Midwives and Health Visitors 1990: para. 88). Again, the reason given was to ease recruitment and retention problems.

The Secretary of State for Education required each of the Interim Advisory Committees to consider what modifications should be made to the system of selective payments to increase flexibility, recruitment and retention, for example, changes to Incentive Allowances with respect to shortages of teachers in key subjects in particular geographical areas (for example, Interim Advisory Committee 1990: para. 1.4).

*Paying for Performance*

Again, it is the Megaw Inquiry that provides a statement of the government's philosophy on performance-related pay as this applies to the public sector, in this instance the civil service. The main arguments in favour of introducing performance-related pay were: the desirability of having an effective means of rewarding good performance and penalising poor performance other than promotion on one hand or demotion and dismissal on the other; the inequity of giving the same financial rewards to the competent and hardworking and the less capable and hardworking; as a substitute for fewer promotion opportunities following reductions in the size of the civil service; finally, because outside organisations have introduced merit pay schemes (Megaw Inquiry 1982: para. 326).

The fact that there has been continuity on this issue of policy is demonstrated by the commitment to PRP in the *Citizen's Charter* which states the government's intention of linking pay in the public sector to a person's contribution to the standard of services via more delegation of decisions on pay rewards to those responsible for the delivery of a service; including performance-related pay as part of the normal package of pay and conditions and ensuring that rewards for performance are only given when demanding quality of service targets have been met. The rationale offered for these changes is that 'the ways in which people are paid can have a powerful effect on improving performance' (Prime Minister's Office 1991: 35).

## Changing the Practice

Successive Conservative governments thus developed a distinctive ideology in respect of public sector pay determination, when seen in the context of the criteria and institutions which they inherited: as they have been in office from 1979 onwards, they have had ample opportunity to effect changes which corresponded with their ideological position and it is to these changes which will now be considered.

At first glance it does appear that public sector pay has undergone significant changes: performance related pay schemes were introduced for civil servants, NHS employees and teachers. Local authority employers also use such schemes. Major groups of public sector employees were removed from collective bargaining. Burnham was disbanded in 1987 and replaced by the Interim Advisory Committee which had similarities to a Review Board but was required to make its recommendations within a global figure given by the Secretary of State. In 1991, the Interim Advisory Committee was itself superseded by the School Teachers Review Body. Nurses, Midwives, Health Visitors and Professions Allied to Medicine were removed from the arena of free collective bargaining in 1983, with the establishment of their Review Body. Several local authorities removed either single or several groups of employees from national agreements. The abolition of the Clegg Commission on Comparability in 1980 neatly indicates the government's view of comparability in public sector wage determination. Reforms of both the NHS and Education have introduced structural changes which either enable organisations to leave national pay bargaining (the establishment of NHS Trusts, grant-maintained schools) or at least introduce greater flexibility into pay units (with district managed units in the NHS and local management of schools(LMS)). NHS Trusts are allowed to negotiate their own pay rates and conditions of service for all staff except junior doctors. Grant-maintained schools will be able to do the same if they choose to withdraw from the scope of the new School Teachers' review body. District Managed Units will have greater freedom in that where new jobs are created locally which are not covered by any central grade definition, managers can pay whatever is appropriate taking account of local labour-market factors (Caines 1991: 14). This freedom is currently being used with Health Care Assistants. With the introduction of LMS, local authorities must delegate control of the schools budget to Governing Bodies which are responsible for appointing and paying staff.

Following the policy initiative announced in the 1988 Cabinet Office paper 'Next Steps', a number of civil service departments have been, completely or partially, hived off into Executive Agencies, e.g. HMSO and both the benefits and contributions sections of the DSS. By July 1991, there were fifty such agencies (Prime Minister's Office 1991: 36). Agencies have autonomy to set their own pay and grading levels.

Thus the picture sketched above is one that would support the view that Conservative governments have transformed public sector pay determination in line with their ideology. However, a closer consideration of these changes does not necessarily sustain this picture.

*Comparability Lives*

As has already been noted, Conservative governments eschewed comparability in the sense of social justice, preferring that rates of pay should be determined by market forces. Thus the Megaw Inquiry, the annual Review Bodies on Doctors' and Dentists' Remuneration, for Nursing Staff, Midwives and Health Visitors and later the Interim Advisory Committee for Teachers were urged to link pay to what was necessary to recruit, retain and motivate staff. Each of these bodies, however, recognised that such objectives would oblige employers to use *external comparisons* in setting pay levels for civil servants, doctors, nurses and teachers. Thus, while Megaw agreed that the key principle for civil servants should be what was needed to recruit, retain and motivate them, the Inquiry also argued that this principle involved a form of comparability in that recruitment and retention had to be underpinned by pay increases and levels of remuneration which 'broadly match those available in the private sector for staff undertaking jobs with *comparable job weight*' (Megaw 1982: para. 101; our emphasis). Not only did Megaw support the use of external comparisons, but the reference to assessment by reference to 'job weight' would appear to involve a commitment to job evaluation, the approach which underpinned the pay research method discussed above.

The 1983 Review Body on Doctors' and Dentists' Remuneration argued that while doctors' and dentists' position in the earnings hierarchy should not be fixed, 'we need to have proper regard to their relative position in the hierarchy' (Review Body on Doctors' and Dentists' Remuneration 1983: para. 12); and it added that one of the considerations of the review was that 'recommendations should not involve any significant change in the existing relationship between doctors and dentists' earnings and those at comparable levels of skill, responsibility and workload in the economy' (ibid.). These views were reiterated the following year. While the Review Body did not subscribe to any concept of comparison which would entail more or less automatic indexation of pay, it maintained that 'Comparisons with remuneration outside the NHS must continue to have some part to play in our considerations' (Review Body on Doctors' and Dentists' Remuneration 1984: para. 12). In 1987, the Review Body suggested that external comparisons were not irrelevant to the work of a Review Body which compensates to some extent for the absence of an independent labour market. Recruitment and retention to the professions within their remit could be seriously affected if they were not properly rewarded (Review Body on Doctors' and Dentists' Remuneration 1987: para. 26).

The Review Body for Nursing Staff, Midwives and Health Visitors, while accepting that it had to take account of the country's economic circumstances and financial constraints, argued that such concerns should not be allowed to override all other considerations (Review Body for Nursing Staff, Midwives and Health Visitors: 1984; 1987; 1989); identification of shortages in geographical areas and particular specialities exposed recruitment and retention principles as unsatisfactory (Review Body for Nursing Staff, Midwives and Health Visitors: 1987; 1988; 1991). On three occassions – 1985, 1987 and 1991 – the Review Body expressed disquiet about the idea that market forces could be used to determine pay in a situation where the NHS was a near monopoly employer. The 1991 statement gives a clear idea of the approach of the Body to public sector pay determination:

> The logic of the argument about market forces would, if applied to this situation suggest that pay levels need be set only marginally above the point at which significant losses would occur from nurses abandoning their profession altogether and seeking other forms of employment. Those who commit themselves to a professional career such as nursing, and eschew industrial action, may reasonably expect that wider considerations than this will be

taken into account in settling their pay. Moreover, the NHS controls the number of training places and therefore the supply of trained staff as well as the demand for them; in such a near monopoly situation, the sufficiency of applicants at any time is an inconclusive test of the adequacy of existing levels. (Review Body for Nursing Staff, Midwives and Health Visitors 1991: para. 30)

The Review Body frequently commissioned the Office of Manpower Economics to carry out surveys of relative pay levels, and such survey results were one of the factors that they considered in making their recommendations. Comparability studies led the Review Body to comment on at least two occasions that levels of remuneration for nurses were modest (Review Body for Nursing Staff, Midwives and Health Visitors 1987; 1988).

Similarly, the Interim Advisory Committee did not disregard comparability. While not advocating automatic rises in line with movements in pay levels outside teaching, its second report in 1989 commented that if increases were below the rate of those enjoyed by other groups, this would contribute to low morale within the profession, a view reiterated in its third report. The fourth and final report of the Interim Advisory Committee pursued this theme: 'While teachers cannot expect automatic comparability with other groups, or periods, neither can they be considered in isolation from the rest of the economy' (Interim Advisory Committee 1991: para. 7.10).

Indeed, these arguments were, *de facto*, accepted by governments whenever they used an indexation formula, which of course represents a form of comparability. Indexation has been retained for both the police and the fire service and the concept extended to the civil service and teachers. For the former, pay is linked to the interquartile range of pay settlements in the private sector, following annual surveys of private-sector pay movements. In the case of teachers, the 1991 remit to the Interim Advisory Committee stated that percentage increases in the total pay bill for 1991–2 'should fall within the interquartile range of the annual percentage movements in the pay of non manual employees outside the public services sector' (Interim Advisory Committee 1991: 7).

*Decentralisation Rules?*

From the earlier discussion, it would appear that significant changes had been made by the government to the practices of public sector pay determination with respect to the decentralisation of pay. However, two dimensions of decentralisation were identified: delegation of decisions on pay to the unit of employment and the introduction of regional variations in pay. On the latter, the government has made no progress.

Megaw opposed regional variations in pay rates, except for the London weighting: the Inquiry pointed to the lack of detailed and reliable information on regional variations in pay for comparable groups of employees; the additional costs and complexity that would be added to the pay system and the fact that the regional boundaries of different departments were not coterminous with one another and that it would be difficult to find boundaries which met the management requirements of all departments (Megaw Inquiry 1982: paras 298–303). The first Interim Advisory Committee on Teachers' Pay was asked to consider regional/local pay and subject differentiation of pay. They rejected such proposals out of hand, pointing out that teaching was a collegiate activity with teachers acting as a team: any variations in pay, beyond some informal differentiation to take account of recruitment and retention needs, would undermine such a concept. The Committee also listed a number of other arguments against the introduction of variations: they would discourage teachers from moving, thus 'local schools would tend to lose any influx of new blood and fresh ideas' (Interim Advisory Committee 1988: para. 5.2.7); they were inflexible and it would be difficult to respond to changes in shortage subjects or labour supply problems in different areas; they would be perceived as unfair by the profession; as the supply of qualified teachers was relatively inelastic, differentials would merely redistribute shortages; finally, such an approach was ineffective because in those subjects where teachers were in relatively short supply e.g. computing, the private sector would always be able to outbid local authorities (ibid.: para. 5.2.8). The Interim Advisory Committee did not change its views in subsequent reports.

The Review Body for Nursing Staff, Midwives and Health Visitors flirted with differential pay, supporting the Health Departments proposals for pilot schemes. However, it also warned against selective pay becoming 'a soft option for poor management' (Review Body for Nursing Staff, Midwives and Health Visitors 1989: para. 115); and stressed the desirability of monitoring whether the supplements had achieved their objectives. The Review Body was also concerned that the supplements should not lead to leapfrogging between districts. In the report of the following year, it noted 'that flexible pay has caused resentment in a number of locations' (Review Body 1990: para. 95) and was far from convinced that any proper measurement of the effects of the scheme had been attempted (ibid.: para 97). The Health Department did not request that the 1991 Review Body extend this pilot project.

However, it would appear that on the other dimension of decentralisation, namely, delegating decisions on pay to the unit of employment, the government has made more progress, with LMS in education, the establishment of Trusts in the NHS and Executive Agencies in the Civil Service.

Under LMS, LEAs are required to delegate to the Governors of each secondary school, and primary school with 200 or more pupils (all primary schools from 1994), the annual budget for running the school. Thus the 'Governing Body will have freedom to deploy resources within the schools budget according to their own educational needs and priorities. They will determine the number of both teaching and non teaching staff at the school' (Department of Education and Science 1988, Circular 7/88: para. 21). However, once the Governing Body has decided on the number of teachers to appoint and at what grade, they must then abide by the national scales of pay. Currently, LEAs have control of discretionary elements of pay, e.g. the option of paying a higher salary than the agreed rates to head/deputy head teachers, discretion to pay an additional allowance to an unqualified teacher. This discretion is to be transferred to individual schools but there is no evidence that in terms of the total teaching budget, the sums involved are more than marginal. Although governors will have greater control over the pay of non-teaching staff, this constitutes, on average, only 9 per cent of a school's budget (Dixon 1991:60).

Grant-maintained schools will have the option of ignoring national pay settlements in favour of locally determined pay (Teachers Pay Act 1991). However, at the end of January 1992 there were only 143 such schools (Treasury 1992a: para. 27).

Within the reformed NHS, Trusts gain considerable autonomy in personnel matters, employing all staff directly, and able to establish their own conditions of service and pay, other than for junior doctors. However, staff who transfer to the Trusts will be able to retain their Whitley/Review Body pay rates as long as they remain in their jobs or are not promoted. Obviously, this provides a constraint in local pay bargaining even with increasing numbers of NHS staff being employed by Trusts, as not all will be on Trust rates of pay.

The evidence on Executive Agencies looks far less contentious. By the end of 1991, there were fifty agencies each determining its own pay and grading levels. Thus decentralisation of pay seems to be securely established in the civil service.

Thus, while movement on decentralisation of pay determination to the unit has been more marked than the attempt to differentiate pay on a regional basis, close analysis of many services shows that a number of caveats still apply. Equally, it is important to bear in mind that government espousal of decentralised pay is at odds with the objective to maintain financial control over many services. Consequently, there is little room for manoeuvre over pay within cash-limited services. If certain groups are paid more, other groups must be paid less: 'winners' are accompanied by 'losers'.

*Performance is All?*

The Megaw Inquiry wholeheartedly supported the government's philosophy on performance-related pay, arguing that the problems in introducing such a scheme into the civil service – that the nature of public-service work required co-operation and shared objectives, the subjectivity of appraisals and significant administrative costs – were not insuperable. However, taking note of the unions' reservations they suggested an evolutionary approach to this change.

Performance-related pay schemes were introduced into most areas of the public sector in the mid-1980s, but they had limited coverage and only a small proportion of the pay bill was allocated to them. In 1991, only 1.5 per cent of teachers were in receipt of Incentives Allowances which are given to reward outstanding classroom ability (Foreman 1991: 9); and by 1989, performance-related pay only extended to 9,000 regional, senior and middle managers in the NHS (Pay and Benefits Bulletin 1989). Local authorities introduced schemes only for certain key professional groups, except where there had been a move away from national bargaining when it then became an integral part of the new arrangements (Income Data Services 1991:41). In addition, the sums involved in such schemes were small. It was estimated that PRP in the NHS in 1988–89 would account for only 0.02 per cent of the total pay bill (Bailey and Trinder 1989:107); and that only 5 per cent of the salary bill for teachers would be spent on Incentive Allowances in 1991–2 (Interim Advisory Committee 1991: 59).

However, in the *Citizen's Charter* the government clearly envisages an increased proportion of total remuneration coming from PRP. Thus Pay Review Bodies will be urged 'to take performance more into account in their recommendations' (Prime Minister's Office 1991: 35). Additional money is not to be made available for this initiative, 'But we will expect the composition of the recommendation to change so that a larger proportion of pay would be linked to performance' (ibid.). Delegation and flexibility are to be encouraged in the civil service; in the NHS (via Trusts) and in education with grant-maintained schools.

Subsequently, newspaper headlines have conveyed the impression that the changes would be farr reaching, for example, 'Nurses told pay to be linked to performance' (*The Times*: 21 November 1991).

However, the 1992 Review Body for Nursing Staff, Midwives and Health Visitors gave no indication as to the proportion of pay which should be related to performance, neither did the Health Departments, beyond suggesting that, in future, the Review Body would be invited to recommend a 'target average percentage pay increase' of which a proportion would be for basic increase payable to all staff and 'the balance would be available for local flexibility, *including performance pay* (Review Body for Nursing Staff, Midwives and Health Visitors 1992: para. 24 ; our emphasis). No additional funding was to be available. Obviously if local labour market supplements absorbed most of this discretionary element in pay, little or indeed none would be available for PRP. (Our thanks to Graham Wells for bringing this point to our attention.)

The Minister for Health had a similar position in her evidence to the Review Body on Doctors' and Dentists' Remuneration. The Chief Executive of the NHS, in turn, offered no precise figure for PRP, merely saying 'that in time he expected to see a larger proportion of the annual pay increase for doctors and dentists devoted to performance pay. Little extra money would be available in this way in the first few years' (Review Body on Doctors' and Dentists' Remuneration 1992: para. 28). The School Teachers' Review Body did not consider the precise balance between basic pay and the performance-related element.

Thus, the case of PRP reflects similar trends to those observed with respect to comparability and decentralisation: in that, there is a disjuncture between dramatic claims and modest changes.


## A Flawed Enterprise: the Case of Performance-Related Pay


So far the argument has concentrated on the government's ideological approach to pay determination and the relation between this approach and its practice. However, another central question involves how viable are individualised approaches to pay bargaining in the public sector. The Review Body on Doctors' and Dentists' Remuneration, for Nursing Staff, the Interim Advisory Committee for Teachers' Pay and its successor, the School Teachers Review Body, have all highlighted the organisational problems of moving towards more individualised form of pay, even when they have been favourably inclined to the government initiatives. This section will explore, in some detail, their discussions with respect to performance-related pay (PRP), the most distinctive form of individualised pay.

PRP can be defined as a means of 'providing for periodic increases in pay which are incorporated into basic salary or wages and which result from assessments of individual performance and personal value to the organisation. Such increases may determine the rate of progression through pay scales or ranges. They are expressed either as percentages of basic pay, as pre-determined (variable) cash increments or as unconsolidated lump sums' (Incomes Data Services/Institute of Personnel Management, quoted in Murlis 1987: 29). Although the details of schemes vary, all have common elements: a system of performance appraisal and assessment and a means of translating performance assessment into financial rewards (or penalties).

Systems linking pay and performance became widespread in the private sector during the early 1980s. Although initially restricted to managerial groups, they were extended rapidly to white-collar and clerical workers (Lewis 1991). The spread of schemes in the public sector and the government's desire to extend their use have already been discussed.

Three major arguments are usually put forward for adopting PRP schemes: they are seen as operating to solve recruitment and retention problems in areas (both geographical and specialist) where there are severe shortages of staff; they offer an additional means of motivating staff, differentiating reward according to effort and thus producing a 'fairer', more equitable system of pay; and they are seen as means of improving performance in the organisation.

At the request of the relevant government departments, the 1992 Review Bodies on Doctors' and Dentists' Remuneration, for Nursing Staff, Midwives and Health Visitors and for School Teachers considered the case for introducing PRP into their respective professional groups. While support ranged from enthusiastic to non-committal, each of the Review Bodies was concerned with the potential problems of implementation. Their dicussions can be taken as exemplars of the problems generally associated with PRP.

*Measuring Up?*

The measurement of performance presents perhaps the most difficult aspect of PRP; this is particularly so in the public sector where the objectives, outcomes and outputs of many services are diverse and unclear.

In oral evidence to the Doctors' and Dentists' Review Body, the Minister of Health conceded, 'that performance was not easy to measure' (Review Body on Doctors' and Dentists' Remuneration 1992: para. 28). The Review Body did not advance beyond suggesting that 'performance should be measured not only by objective factors like output and unit costs, but also by subjective factors like the perceptions by patients of the quality of service they receive' (ibid.: para. 34). They concluded that in most areas of medicine and dentistry the process of assessing and rewarding performance was rudimentary (ibid.: para. 36). These comments raise similar issues to those discussed in chapter 2: the idea of operating with a range of performance measures would run into the difficulty that it is hard to see how any composite measure of performance could be generated when such heterogeneous measures are used. Given this, there is a distinct possibility of PRP being attached to indicators, such as reductions in waiting-lists or increases in the number of patients treated. Thus, PRP could be used as a means of meeting political targets, rather than achieving service improvements. In the case of health, for example, the use of activity-based criteria, with the emphasis on throughput, could undermine quality of care and disadvantage patients with more complicated time-consuming conditions.

The Review Body on Nursing Staff, Midwives and Health Visitors did not discuss substantive issue surrounding PRP: however, they did note the reservation expressed by staff about how the quality of care could be measured in a clinical environment.

The School Teachers' Review Body, which wholeheartedly supported a properly designed PRP scheme accepted that the major problem was in developing effective arrangements, in particular deciding on the criteria and method for judging teachers' performance, especially in the absence of systematic performance indicators for schools. While the DES had published indicators which could be used by schools for internal management purposes, the Review Body rejected these for PRP schemes, arguing that they were 'concerned with inputs and process, and require subject assessments' (School Teachers' Review Body 1992: para. 65).

The DES suggested in its evidence that quantitative information, such as results in public examinations, destinations of school leavers, truancy rates and results in the national curriculum assessments would be used. However, not all of these will apply to primary schools, and the introduction of national curriculum assessments will not be completed until 1996. Notwithstanding all this, the Review Body announced its intention of developing proposals and indicators focusing specifically on improvements in, rather than absolute levels of school performance, so that a scheme of PRP could be introduced in 1993/4.

Most PRP literature addresses the problem that although the financial reward is linked to individual performance, it is frequently difficult to isolate the performance of an individual from that of others in the organisation, objectives being achieved through teamwork or co-operation. Recognising this problem, the Doctors' and Dentists' and School Teachers' Review Bodies suggest that rewards should be given at a group level, the former suggesting that this 'may be easier to introduce and measure' (Review Body for Doctors' and Dentists' Remuneration 1992: para. 34). However, no evidence is produced to substantiate this statement and it is just as likely that measuring *group* performance will be dogged by precisely the same problems as measuring *individual* performance.

The School Teachers' Review Body aimed to combine group and individual assessment of performance by suggesting that in the first instance pay increases should be related to the performance of each school rather than individual teachers, thus recognising that teaching is a collegiate activity. However, it then follows that mechanisms must be found for translating the rewards into pay for individual teachers. They question whether governing bodies should have discretion to give different rewards 'to those teachers they judge to have contributed most to the improvement in the school's performance' (School Teachers' Review Body 1992: para. 76). The notion that an individual's contribution to a group effort can be separately distinguished and rewarded raises two major problems in any PRP scheme, namely, how to ensure equity and fairness in the distribution of rewards and the implications for the organisation when this fails. Furthermore, group rewards undermine the whole rationale for PRP which is a strategy to motivate *individuals*, a position which the School Teachers' Review Body recognises very clearly.

*Paying Up?*

The Departments of Health and the DES made it clear in their evidence to their respective Review Bodies that there was to be no additional money available for PRP. Both Review Bodies expressed concern at this: the Doctors' and Dentists' Review Body stating, 'performance-related pay schemes present fundamental challenges to pay systems which limit overall earnings' (Review Body on Doctors' and Dentists' Remuneration 1992: para. 31). Unlike the private sector where higher earnings can be funded by increased sales, this is not possible in the NHS, where the service is free to the consumer within a fixed budget. Thus improved performance of staff might result not in reduced costs but an expansion of free services, with cost savings arising only in the future with improved standards of health (ibid.: para 32). The Review Body concluded 'that the incentive impact of performance-related pay schemes will be weakened if increased payments for performance are seen as being automatically set off against future pay rises' (ibid.: para. 33).

A similar argument is put forward by the School Teachers' Pay Review Body, namely that a PRP scheme 'would be more effective and offer greater motivation to teachers if the Government were to make additional funds available' (School Teachers' Review Body 1992: para. 75). This may be so, but the critical point is that the Department announced its intention of introducing a PRP scheme which was not dependent on the availability of additional money. Obviously, there is a concern with controlling costs of PRP. Any scheme must address this problem and there are three main mechanisms for doing so: a forced distribution (or quota) which limits the numbers of staff who can receive payments; a fixed budget, where there is maximum amount of money available for payments in any one year; and, incorporating PRP within the existing budget, which is favoured by the Departments. In such a case money for PRP can only be found if savings are produced elsewhere: PRP is then dependent on the organisation operating more 'efficiently' and 'effectively'. In all these instances there is a clear tension between the desire to create an inducement to improved 'performance' and the fact that finite resources limit either the numbers who can qualify or the size of the reward.

*Achieving What?*

The government is an enthusiastic supporter of PRP and intends to extend its application. Given this commitment it is essential to evaluate this strategy. Does it achieve its objectives?

The seventeen local authorities surveyed by the Local Authorities Conditions of Service Advisory Board (LACSAB) claimed that PRP had assisted recruitment and retention, but they qualified this in two ways. First, that it was difficult to say that PRP alone had eased labour supply problems because it was part of a pay and bargaining package: thus other elements of the package – assistance with housing, car leasing – could have been more significant. Second, even if PRP did have a positive impact, this was likely to be short-term, as neighbouring authorities would adopt similar schemes and possibly set off an inflationary wages spiral (LACSAB 1990: 60).

In linking pay to performance, PRP is predicated on a particular motivational theory, namely that there is a relationship between reward and effort. However, research provides little support for such a simplistic approach; rather it emphasises that there are many motives which influence people at work – job satisfaction, commitment, etc., and that money was rarely the most important. In their study of nine organisations, Kessler and Purcell (1992: 27) found that many managers were sceptical of any link between pay and performance.

If the motivational theory underlying PRP is suspect, it follows that its effect on the performance of an organisation is likely to be questionable. The LACSAB study found that few of the local authorities it surveyed 'had attempted to verify whether linking pay to individual employee performance was having a beneficial impact on the efficiency and effectiveness of council services' (LACSAB 1990: 54). Indeed, the local authorities had either ignored this or dismissed it as too difficult an exercise. The beneficial consequences of PRP in improving performance was a matter of faith.

Kessler and Purcell came to similar conclusions. None of the companies in their research had developed criteria for judging the success of PRP in terms of improvement in company performance; indeed, none of them expected there to be a clear connection. As Kessler and Purcell comment, 'the link between pay and performance remains as obscure as ever' (Kessler and Purcell 1992: 29).

If a 'not proven' verdict can be returned on these stated objectives (i.e. recruitment and retention, motivation and improvement of performance), then it is necessary to look elsewhere for the rationale of the schemes. Kessler and Purcell situate PRP within a strategy for promoting organisational change, and within such a context it fulfils three objectives: PRP, with its focus on 'performance' can be a means of facilitating change in organisational culture, a point made by the Chief Executive of the NHS in his evidence to the 1992 Review Body on Doctors' and Dentists' Remuneration. While accepting that initially little money would be tied up in PRP for doctors, he stated that in the short term 'it was the cultural change involved in introducing performance pay that was so important' (Review Body on Doctors' and Dentists' Remuneration 1992: para. 28). Equally, as PRP is an individualistic form of remuneration it can be used to weaken trade union influence in pay bargaining and, because performance appraisal (a key component of PRP) inevitably involves a degree of subjectivity, it can form the basis for extending management discretion and control over the employee. Finally, PRP can be linked to financial control in that it targets pay and thus provides 'value for money', unlike across-the-board automatic annual increments (Kessler and Purcell 1992 : 21–3).

Kessler and Purcell conclude that PRP is not a neutral technique for determining pay; indeed, this conclusion could be taken further by arguing that PRP exemplifies the managerialist ideology, discussed in chapter 1, an ideology whose focus is on control of the individual by a management hierarchy emphasising accountability through the setting of targets. The appeal of PRP is not so much related to its demonstrable success in improving organisational performance but to its consistency with the precepts of managerialism favoured by the Conservative governments of the 1980s.

# Conclusion

Conservative governments consistently argued against the institutions and criteria for determining public sector pay which they inherited from both their Labour and Conservative predecessors. A robust attack was launched on comparability, incomes policies and national pay bargaining in favour of individualised, flexible negotiations. A strong impression was created that here was an area where governments had made considerable inroads into past practices; yet an evaluation of the policies on public sector pay suggests a rather more complex story.

The Review Bodies for Doctors and Dentists, and for Nurses, Midwives and Health Visitors were requested by the Health Departments to base their recommendations for annual increases on what was necessary to recruit, retain and motivate staff. However, they recognised that such exhortations did not engender realistic prescriptions and that pay for doctors, dentists and nurses must be seen in the context of the wider labour market. Thus the recommendations of these Review Bodies invariably took account of external comparisons: yet only once did the government reject a recommendation outright, in 1989, when it refused to increase the size of the A distinction award for consultants. In accepting these recommendations, therefore, the government accepted the notion of comparability. Indeed, with the remit given to the 1991 Interim Advisory Committee on Teachers' Pay and Conditions it specifically required the Committee to take comparability into account by indexing teachers' pay to the interquartile range of percentage movements in the pay of private-sector non-manual employees (see p. 120 above).

Acceptance of the Review Body mechanism *per se*, is an intriguing feature of Conservative pay policy. Given their commitment to devolving pay determination to employers and employees, it seems odd that they should have not only tolerated third-party independent bodies but indeed, increased their number – in 1983 for Nurses, Midwives and Health Visitors and 1991 for Teachers, so that approximately 1.5 million public sector employees have their pay determined by Review Bodies. However, Review Bodies are a useful device for governments driven by an ideology of the market, yet still needing to control public spending. Review Bodies can make their recommendations, but governments can reject them, or more likely, stage them. This was particularly true for the doctors and dentists. Between 1984 and 1991, the Review Bodies' recommendations for these groups were paid in full on only one occasion, leading the Review Bodies to protest, in their 1983 and 1987 reports, that such an interventionist stance was difficult to reconcile with the supposed independence of the Review Board system. Review Bodies allow a combination of an arm's length relationship with the government, with the possibility of governmental modification of the final pay award to take account of 'affordability'. Indeed, the Director of Personnel in the NHS has admitted that abolition of the NHS pay review bodies is no longer a government priority (Financial Times 9 November 1992).

Of course, governments had not been averse to cruder, more direct forms of intervention to overturn agreements between employer and employee. An example of this is the government's refusal to accept the pay settlement for university lecturers for 1992–3. The Committee of Vice Chancellors and Principals was required by the Department of Education and Science to reduce this from 6 per cent to an across- the board settlement of 4.25 per cent with the additional money being used for PRP (*Guardian* 17 July 1992). However, Review Bodies allow such direct tactics to resorted to in a more sparing way.

Governments were anxious to increase local pay flexibility. While there was little progress on the issue of regional pay, there was a stronger trend to functional decentralisation, that is devolving pay bargaining to the level of the unit, for example, Trusts, Executive Agencies, grant-maintained schools. This, however, gives a spurious independence to the unit. First, as Brown and Rowthorn (1990) point out, this form of decentralisation makes sense 'only in so far as the separate functions are truly independently accountable' and this would require the units, in linking pay, efficiency and quality to be able to have their own financial and performance targets (Brown and Rowthorn 1990:13). However, this was not the case with the units created in health, education and the civil service Executive Agencies, where targets were set by the government.

Second, the decentralised units still remained part of the provision of a national service, where the government retained centralised financial control.

Third, although the government maintained that they were giving Trusts, schools, etc., increased flexibility to determine wages at the unit level, it could not force them to act independently. This was illustrated by the example of forty-two hospital units in the West Midlands, which formed a consortium to develop a purpose-built job evaluation system (Millar 1992: 15). Obviously, one of the objectives of this move was to prevent units, which would be competing for the same staff, leapfrogging one another.

Government policies on public pay determination in the 1980s were marked by incoherence and a disjuncture of rhetoric and reality. However, in one area successive governments *did* pursue a consistent policy and that was in respect of the differential treatment meted out to groups of public sector employees. According to Brown and Rowthorn's analysis of the New Earnings Survey data, doctors, nurses and police constables achieved an increase in their real earnings of 26 per cent, 38 per cent and 26 per cent over the period 1981–9 a period in which the overall earnings of all employees rose by 25 per cent. Teachers fared badly, the worst affected being those in further and higher education with increases of 6 per cent and 5 per cent respectively. The smallest increases in real weekly earnings were for hospital porters (4 per cent), hospital orderlies (3 per cent) and refuse collectors (5 per cent). As Brown and Rowthorn state, 'the position of these groups deteriorated far more than that of the unskilled in the economy as a whole' (Brown and Rowthorn 1990: 7) Undoubtedly, a key element here was CT and CCT.

Brown and Rowthorn conclude that although certain groups experienced favourable treatment, public sector employees as a whole saw their relative position decline in the 1980s. Employees who fared worst were the least educated, a high proportion of whom were women (ibid.). Such a conclusion is in stark contrast to the executives in the newly privatised industries (and the private sector generally) where ideas of the 'going rate' and comparability were not regarded as 'outmoded concepts'.

# 6

## Conclusion: A Future that Will Fail? Managerialism and Consumerism in the Nineties

In this final chapter the aim is to bring together the themes developed in the book and to relate them to trends in the 1990s. The argument is divided into four sections: the first summarises the conclusions of the first five chapters by relating the substantive changes discussed in the book to the concept of public sector managerialism proposed in chapter 1. The second attempts to situate welfare politics in the 1990s with respect to the legacy of the 1980s; this involves both a discussion of Conservative politics under John Major and Labour's response to its electoral failure in the last four general elections. The section concludes that there is, in a very real sense, a consensus between the two major parties, a consensus that covers the framework within which economic policy is to be conducted and extends to the way in which public sector services are expected to be run. The argument put forward is that this is not a benign consensus. The third section identifies what we see as the central defects of the position shared by both Conservative and Labour Parties. Finally, the fourth section sketches an alternative agenda for public sector services.

### The Legacy of the 1980s

In chapter 1 it was argued that the legacy of Conservative politics in the 1980s was an ambiguous one. Following Mrs Thatcher's election as Conservative leader in 1975, an ideological shift occurred in which many themes of the New Right were taken up avidly. In particular, demand management was repudiated, unemployment was seen as a supply-side problem, and a proposals to restrict the rights of trade unions were formulated. Many of these aspects were carried over into policy on collective and individual labour law and in the priority accorded to the control of inflation over the reduction in unemployment.

However, when it came to policy on the social services, New Right positions were decisively repudiated: privatisation operated only marginally; the principal social services remained state-funded, and state dominance of provision was retained. There were no attempts to introduce consumerist measures such as vouchers. Not surprisingly, New Right authors were disenchanted with Conservative welfare politics, a feature exemplified by Green's (1990) criticisms of the NHS reforms (see chapter 1).

What was central to Conservative welfare politics was managerialism. Government and/or government agencies operated as a *de facto* 'head office', while treating providers as a series of 'operational units'. Targets were set, units monitored, and agencies like the Audit Commission and the National Audit Office were created to diffuse 'good practice'.

This politics is reflected in the substantive areas which we have discussed in chapters 2–5. Performance measures were developed and this was predominantly a top-down exercise in which the emphasis was on government or government agencies developing the criteria by which units were to be judged. Equally, formally independent bodies like the Audit Commission shared the basic managerialist assumptions prevalent in central government (McSweeney 1988).

Quasi-markets might appear to inject a greater degree of decentralisation allowing operational units to define their own objectives and mix of activities. However, such powers were, in fact, quite circumscribed: in higher education purchasing was centralised and the policy of the purchasing agencies closely aligned with government priorities such as the aim to increase numbers while driving down unit costs; quality control was not a matter for purchaser and provider but involved a monitoring role for government departments and agencies; the quasi-market in health was 'managed' from the centre so that politically unacceptable results did not occur.

In the case of CCT the role of head office was even more salient. The regulatory framework sought to control the process of tendering and of tender evaluation. The Department of Health and the Department of the Environment could wield coercive powers where it was suspected that the centrally determined rules had been broken. The rhetoric of competition was used, but the fine print included conditions which loaded the dice in favour of the private contractor.

Policy statements on pay determination used the jargon of the market but the practice was managerialist. The scope of third-party intervention was sharply increased by extending the role of Review Bodies in pay determination to nurses, midwives, health visitors and teachers. Head Office could keep its distance but also extend discretion to accept, reject or stage. Public sector pay determination was complex and involved different forms for different groups, politics was in command.

In all these cases there was a symbiotic relationship between the creation of unit autonomy, via Trusts, LMS, DSOs, Executive Agencies and polytechnics with corporate status, and central control. This was not a policy of decentralisation or marketisation; it was centralisation with a limited degree of operational autonomy.

Equally, managerialism was not politically neutral. In chapter 1 it was argued that a particularly important point where managerialist and New Right positions were congruent was over the critique of producer groups. Again, such trends feature in the substantive areas of policy. Performance measurement was used, admittedly in a rather variable way, to discipline professionals: teachers were to be rendered accountable for school examination results; the research efforts of university lecturers were to be ranked. The regulatory framework around CCT brutally and explictly attacked organised labour. Performance-related pay was introduced. Conservative ideology on pay determination stressed an individualised approach to the employment relationship.

## Majorism and the Labour Party: the Double Consensus?

Mrs Thatcher resigned from the leadership of the Conservative in November 1990. At that time there was considerable speculation as to whether her successor, John Major, would abandon or continue her policies. The publication in July 1991 of the White Paper *The Citizen's Charter*, clearly an initiative of John Major's, provides an opportunity to judge how far there is likely to be continuity in Conservative welfare politics.

There are four main themes in *The Citizen's Charter*: a commitment to improving the *quality* of public services; *choice* as 'the best spur to quality improvement'; *standards* to be public so that a citizen can act where a service is unacceptable; and *value* for money for the taxpayer (Prime Minister's Office 1991: 45).

A central feature of the *Charter* is that individual units – for example, schools or hospitals – should publish information on their performance for service users and that this should be produced in a form which allows comparison of performance. Thus, 'Targets should be published together with full and audited information about the results achieved.Whenever possible, information should be in comparable form, so that there is pressure to emulate the best' (ibid.: 5).

For health, the NHS Management Executive 'will set out the main areas, in which local standards must be set, monitored and published on a consistent national basis' (ibid.: 11). Similarly in education, central government 'will lay a duty on LEAs to disseminate and publish information in accordance with a standard format' (ibid.: 14). A final example can be taken from social services, where nationally promulgated quality standards are to be available as a benchmark (ibid.: 21).

A range of mechanisms for delivering quality services are to be pursued: for example, contracting out, which, it is claimed, not only insures good-quality services but does so at a lower cost (ibid.: 33); and competitive tendering which 'has raised standards of performance' (ibid.: 34). In the same vein, the scope of 'performance testing' and performance-related pay is to be extended (ibid.: 33). Newly constituted inspectorates are to be opened up to lay members so 'that judgement of what represents good practice is not just left to the professionals' (ibid.: 40). Volunteer lay adjudicators, whose personal qualities would be 'more important than legal expertise or public sector experience', would look into cases where complaints have been ignored and advise people on existing complaints procedure (ibid.: 44). Finally, if a unit such as a hospital could not meet deadlines, purchasers could seek provision elsewhere, 'including if appropriate from the independent sector' (ibid.: 47).

Much has been made of the distinctive nature of the *Charter*, with its apparent emphasis on rights, entitlement, rehabilitation of the public sector. Thus, it has been claimed that it could not have been produced when Mrs Thatcher was in office (see, for example, Miller and Peroni 1992, for press responses to the *Charter*).

What might appear different here is that the negative view of the public sector often associated with Mrs Thatcher is not present. Equally, there is the use of the seductive term 'citizenship', which conjures up images of economic and social rights within a universal welfare state. However, if the *Charter* is set in the context of the discussion earlier in the book, it is clear that the Thatcherite agenda continues. All the ingredients of managerialism are here: the presciptions for targets are laid down from the centre; regulated competition with a strong anti-producer-group emphasis in the paean to competitive tendering; rewards and penalties for good and poor performing units.

# A Consensus on Managerialism?

Particularly since the swing of the Conservatives to a New Right-inflected ideology, a sharp point of difference between the Labour and Conservative Parties has often been seen to lie in social policy. However, Labour has lost the last four general elections and its reaction to such losses, particularly since 1987, has been to move towards the right. This is significant for the framework within which public sector management and welfare politics is discussed because it means that politics in the 1990s may be a question merely of variations on a theme. In this section, we shall examine the consensus on public sector services around agreement on the virtues of managerialism. The argument will examine the Labour manifestos of 1987 and 1992 as key documents which reveal the 'party's ideological home base' (Laver 1984: 34).

## *Labour, Welfare and the 1987 Manifesto*

In the 1987 manifesto the Labour Party's approach to social policy could be seen to exhibit a continuity with traditional Labour commitments to the welfare state. Thus, the section of the manifesto that discusses social welfare is prefaced by the remark that a future Labour government will broaden and deepen the liberty of all individuals and provide the material circumstances and opportunities in which they can make effective choices. In a manner at variance with the New Right, Labour interpreted these commitments as meaning the development of 'collective provision for private use' (Labour Party 1987: 8).

In line with this position, commitments were made to reduce NHS waiting-lists, cut prescription charges and reward nurses and other staff fairly. On community care, the manifesto appreciates the role of 'voluntary efforts which supplement [statutory] services' (ibid.: 9.) There is a recognition of the contribution of informal carers, and a proposal to introduce a carer's allowance. In education the Party committed itself to improve nursery education and expand post-school education. There were references to aspects with managerialist overtones such as the introduction of profiles of achievement, recording individual pupil progress. However, in general, the main concern is with the identification of welfare needs and the development of policies to meet them.

## *Labour in 1992: the Conversion to Managerialism*

The 1992 manifesto is a very different document. It is true that there is some continuity with its predecessor: for example, the commitment to end what they saw as the privatisation of the NHS and policies to expand provision of nursery-school places and to expansion of higher education. There is also a commitment to spend additional money on both the NHS and education, £1 billion and £600 million over a period of 22 months. In the context of traditional Labour approaches to social policy, certain features of the document offer no surprises: for example, the return of opted-out hospitals and schools to health authority and local education authority control. Beyond such commitments, however, the manifesto moves on to a different terrain from that of its predecessor, adopting the language and ideas of its opponent – targets, monitoring, performance.

Thus, a future Labour government would 'create a modern efficient health service with incentives to improve performance' (Labour Party 1992: 16). A Health Quality Commission would 'monitor the quality of care and raise standards, (ibid.: 16).

Care of the elderly and sick would have a higher priority than under the Conservatives. To achieve this change in direction Performance Agreements, which would set local targets, would be negotiated with each health authority and an Incentive Fund would reward those authorities that performed well. Hospital managers would be accountable for meeting their targets but otherwise be given maximum freedom of decision-making (ibid.: 16).

In education, a major concern is both to raise standards and to guarantee that they remain of an acceptable standard. The former objective is to be secured via a Reading Standards Programme and national tests, and the latter by the creation of an Education Standards Committee, which will 'monitor the performance of every school' (ibid.: 18). If a school is underperforming, the Commission will have powers to ensure that it is brought up to standard. Home-school contracts will tell parents both what they can expect from the school and what are their obligations. Parents may call on the Commission if they are dissatisfied with a Local Education Authority or school and 'get action taken' (ibid.: 18). Local Management of Schools, albeit reformed, will continue, and schools will be 'free to manage their day to day budgets, with local education authorities given a new strategic role' (ibid.: 18). Equally, the role of voluntary organisations now moves from supplementing the statutory sector to 'playing a key role in developing services' (ibid.: 20).

By 1992 two of the central themes of Conservative welfare politics, managerialism and consumerism, had been embraced by the Labour Party.

## Consensus on Economic Policy: Cuts in Unemployment, not Full Employment

The shift in policy and ideology under the Conservatives with respect to economic policy centred on the Hayekian themes of the priority of the control of inflation and the definition of unemployment as a supply-side problem. The superordinate role accorded to controlling inflation is another point of continuity between Majorism and Thatcherism. Thus the 1992 Conservative Manifesto argues that: 'When inflation falls, industry can plan again for a profitable future, inflation is attacked on the grounds that 'it destroys jobs' (Conservative Party 1992: 6). In the early 1980s Labour economic policy was quite distinct from such positions and was identified with what came to be known as the Alternative Economic Strategy (AES). While the AES appeared in a number of variants, a common feature was a commitment to reflationary policies and a willingness to contemplate measures such as import controls to underpin such an employment-creation policy. This would have involved, at the very least, a confrontation with the European Commission as a vital element of the Treaty of Rome is the commitment to free trade between member states (K. Williams et al. 1992: 12).

However, by the lead into the 1992 election Labour was adopting a very different stance. At this stage it was fully reconciled to EC membership but it was not so much this fact as its relationship to EC membership and what it tells us about Labour economic policy that is crucial.

After Britain joined the Exchange Rate Mechanism (ERM) of the European Monetary System a frequent line of argument was that it had entered the ERM with an overvalued currency relative to the Deutschmark, going in at a central rate of 2.95DM to the pound. Such a potential threat to British competitiveness and employment might have been expected to have concerned Labour given its traditional emphasis on maximising employment.

However, neither membership of the ERM nor the DM parity was an issue for Labour. In an interview published in the *Financial Times* (27 September 1991), John Smith, then Shadow Chancellor, committed Labour to maintaining the 2.95 parity. This commitment was further embodied in the 1992 Labour manifesto: 'to curb inflation Labour will maintain the value of the pound within the European Exchange Rate Mechanism' (Labour Party 1992: 12). In the *Financial Times* interview Smith also made some revealing remarks with respect to his view of the role of macro-economic policy: 'the overriding purpose of macro-economic policy is economic stability...With stable interest rates and stable exchange rates, we are likely to get investment to flourish' (cited in K. Williams et al. 1992: 17).

Given such a stance it is not surprising that Labour employment policy is cautious. In the 1992 manifesto Labour claimed that it was determined to make a 'swift reduction in unemployment' (Labour Party 1992: 12). However, there is no hint of the term 'full employment' and no target for such reductions.

# Criticising the Consensus

The argument has already shown that both the Labour and Conservative Parties have embraced managerialism and that it is central to their welfare politics. However, the argument developed earlier involves a clear indictment of managerialism. This can be summarised under three headings: the viability of the positive claims of managerialism; the role of managerialism in obscuring genuine political choices; and the abstraction of managerialism.

## Managerialism

Managerialism involves two claims: that the adoption of appropriate managerial structures and techniques will generate standards of performance by which providers can be judged; and that such approaches will improve 'efficiency' and generate 'savings'. The argument developed earlier throws doubt on both these claims. In chapter 2, it was pointed out that the attempt to develop norms of performance runs into problems not just of the measurement of outputs but also the incommensurable dimensions of performance. Since, for example, the E's (economy, efficiency and effectiveness) relate to diverse aspects of 'performance', it is hard to see how one can say that a given local hospital or local-authority provider is 'performing' better than another. Equally, the difficulty with output measurement means that it is usually unclear what 'efficiency' means. If there is no clear definitions of output, how can inputs be related to product? This allows a crude slide whereby output is reduced to throughput and mendacious claims are made that if more students are obtaining degrees or patients treated within a given budget, then an 'efficiency' gain has been achieved. Finally, 'savings' are just as problematic. It is often unclear what is being compared and the term is effectively referring to redistribution of costs: from hospital budgets to informal carers when average length of stay is reduced; from council budgets to cleaners and dustmen when 'tough' management is introduced under CCT.

This leads us to the second problem. Managerialism is dubious because it can hide genuine differences in ideology and political values. Thus, the redistribution of costs referred to above does raise genuine political issues, issues that have long been the stuff of political debate. Thus, there have always been conflicts about the proper role of public services. On the political right the argument was advanced that public services should merely aim at minimum provision, while on the political left the aim of 'universalising the best' was often cited. Equally, there are genuine political divisions on the respective interests of producers and consumers. Managerialist approaches tend to hide such choices. Thus, for example, at its most blatant, as in the case of some of the Cost Improvement Programmes investigated in the King's Fund research, straightforward cuts in service are being represented as efficiency savings (King's Fund 1988). In these cases managerialism involves a bogus redescription of a political question.

The final difficulty with managerialism involves its abstraction. Central to the whole approach is the fact that it claims to be applicable to a wide range of activities. Yet this often means that the precriptions are circular. Thus, if we ask how service standards are to be improved, we are referred to the prescriptions of the model, set targets, contract out, and so on. Not only does this render the discourse empty, it can also compromise the pursuit of the activity. Thus, in the chapter on quasi-markets it was argued that a general model of contractual relations was based on a misunderstanding of the diversity of voluntary-sector provision in community care and that it threatened to *constrain* the range of provision available, a danger that appears to have materialised in the United States. Similarly, in the case of higher education, managerialist approaches have encouraged viewing teaching and research as distinct 'products' and in turn differentiating institutions and staff into research or teaching roles. Yet, arguably, this threatens to undermine the whole distinctive character of higher education in that it involves a critical reflection on the subjects studied, and that a precondition here is that research and teaching are related activities.

## Consumerism

As was shown, in particular in the chapter on quasi-markets, the extent to which consumerism has influenced practice under the Conservatives is limited. However, the *Citizen's Charter* is an illustration of the extent to which consumerist rhetoric is pervasive in the public services. Another interesting feature of the consensus on welfare politics is the extent to which the political left has taken the consumer/customer to its heart. The 1992 Labour manifesto represents one manifestation of this. Others can be found in Michael Meacher's *Diffusing Power: the Key to the Socialist Revival* and publications of the Insitute of Public Policy Research, for example, Blackstone et al.'s *Next Left: an Agenda for the 1990s*. The authors of the latter argue that 'welfare services succeeded in achieving basic levels of provision but were not flexible enough truly to empower people, and too many parts of the public sector paid insufficient heed to the needs of citizens as consumers' (Blackstone et al. 1992: 5).

Commitment to the consumer/customer, however, is not without its problems. These are twofold: what can be termed 'technical' problems, which would need to be considered by any group or political party which espoused the notion; and conceptual problems, which would exercise those who have a commitment to a universalist approach to welfare.

The technical difficulties stem from the fact, raised in chapter 2, that 'consumers' cannot be assumed to be a homogeneous group: thus demands for health care, community care, etc., will come from different groups of consumers. Once this is recognised, the potential for conflict is obvious. Thus, referring to the 'consumer' takes us no further in resolving conflicts or setting priorities.

A more fundamental conceptual problem is that a commitment to consumerism sits uneasily with support for collective provision, universality and citizenship rights, and as such is likely to present problems for the Labour Party, which still maintains a commitment to such ideals.

A key problem with consumerism in this respect is that it implies a homogeneity in the relation to the supplying organisation, be it university, hospital or supermarket. Yet this is clearly false. A student who embarks on a higher-education course has not and cannot expect a guarantee that he or she will graduate. A patient is not in a position to demand that any operation be performed since any decision will be mediated through the professional judgement of the doctor, who may refuse to perform an operation on the grounds of danger to the patient. Such concerns are not relevant when a supermarket sells potentially life-threatening goods like cigarettes to a customer. All that is at issue is whether the customer can pay.

A further problem is the contradiction between the consumer on the one hand and the citizen on the other. The extract quoted from the IPPR document slides one into the other, but this misses a distinct dimension of citizenship as it relates to social policy. In a discussion of social welfare, Richard Titmuss argued that it had 'an integrative objective which is an essential characteristic distinguishing [it] from economic policy...it is thus profoundly concerned with questions of personal identity...' (Titmuss 1968: 131). A position such as this meant that social welfare institutions needed to be judged with respect to their role in social integration. Thus, for example, on this basis it would be desirable for schools, universities and council estates to contain a mix of social groups. The rationale was to generate social integration so that the service was not identified as a residual one, and so that the social mix would strengthen the social solidarity involved in citizenship. Such objectives are not compatible with consumerism, where the relationship to the service is an individualistic one.

### The Inflation Priority

The argument developed earlier suggested that another key element of the consensus was the priority accorded to the control of inflation over the creation of full employment. Part of the basis for this argument is the claim that the control of inflation is a *sine qua non* for the attainment of other key economic goals, including reductions in unemployment. An argument to this effect from the 1992 Conservative manifesto was cited earlier and, while Labour has not expressed it in such blunt terms, it is in line with the logic of their position. The roots of this position in Hayek were demonstrated in chapter 1, and the centrality of the control of inflation to the promotion of lower unemployment has been consistently argued by Conservative politicians. The Conservative 1992 manifesto echoes positions in Mrs Thatcher's first term. Thus, for example, Leon Brittan, then Chief Secretary to the Treasury, argued in a Commons debate in 1981 that 'past inflation has been the cause of present unemployent' (cited in Bootle 1981: 25).

However, such claims, as Bootle has shown, are spurious. He argues that the links between unemployment and inflation can be conceptualised in three ways: (1) as a function of variations in inflation so that the unit costs of high-inflation countries are pushed to a level where they are uncompetitive internationally thus creating job loss; (2) through a negative impact on profits or the creation of a climate of uncertainly with respect to future inflation, which may have the effect of depressing investment; and (3) via the impact on consumers increasing saving in order to rebuild the real value of their savings which have been eroded by inflation, the so-called 'real balance' effect.

All these postulated links are questionable. There is no invariant link between variable levels of inflation between countries and loss of competitiveness. This is *inter alia* because unit costs will vary, not just with domestic cost levels but also with the exchange rate. Thus devaluations can accommodate for higher domestic costs (on the British experience on this point, see Neale 1992). Conversely, low domestic inflation can be associated with a deterioration in international competitiveness. Thus, international investors were attracted by the very low level of Swiss inflation in 1978 (1 per cent at the time) but currency inflows led to a 34 per cent appreciation of the Swiss franc in the period to September of that year.

The postulated link between low investment and high inflation is also problematic. This is because high levels of inflation are not necessarily associated with low profit levels as a share of value added. Thus, Bootle points out that, in 1980, when inflation was *falling*, the share of wages in domestic income in the United Kingdom was *rising* and the share of profits *falling* (Bootle 1981: 27). It has also been argued that high levels of inflation have a depressing effect on investment because they involve high *nominal* interest rates. The argument here is that such high rates are needed to compensate lenders for the erosion of the principal. The potential danger for the borrower arises from the effect of variable levels of inflation over time, since a fall in inflation increases the real burden of borrowing. Such uncertainties are thus seen as a disincentive to invest. However, this argument abstracts from the scope to develop indexed savings vehicles, which both protect the lender and fix the liability of the borrower. Equally, the argument presupposes that high levels of inflation are associated with high variability in inflation rates yet the empirical evidence for this contention is weak (Bootle 1981: 35).

Finally, it is plausible that 'real balance' effects will depress consumption levels. However, this does not prevent government taking a whole series of measures to offset such a reduction in consumption. In this sense there is no inevitable link to unemployment.

Part of the Hayekian argument is that inflation, as an effect of Keynesian demand management policies, operates to weaken economic disciplines and depress overall levels of economic performance. Yet there is no convincing evidence for such claims: as Bootle points out, the relationship between inflation and economic growth is a complex one, but, reviewing evidence from the period 1967–77, he shows that high inflation is not an obstacle to growth *per se*. Thus, the country with the fastest growth rate in his set was Brazil, with an average 7.3 per cent per annum rate of growth; it also had the highest inflation at 26.6 per cent per annum on average. His study found a mix of experience, with relatively high-inflation countries experiencing relatively high growth (Spain) and low growth (United Kingdom) and low-inflation countries experiencing high growth (Austria, Belgium) and low growth (United States, Switzerland) (Bootle 1981: 43). Therborn (1986) found a similar random relationship when he looked at growth in unemployment levels over the decade 1973–83 in relation to inflation: above-average increases in unemployment occurred in relatively low-inflation countries (Germany, Netherlands) and high-inflation countries (United Kingdom); the growth in unemployment was relatively low in Italy with a very high rate of inflation, and very low in Switzerland with a very low rate of inflation (Therborn 1986: 49). This is not to say that inflation does not have distributional implications which present social problems, but that it is not the master economic problem from which success or failure in all other respects flow.

## An Alternative Agenda

In this final section we shall sketch some alternative directions to the consensus which we have identified in this conclusion. In particular, the focus is on the uncritical acceptance, by the Labour Party and by many authors on the political left, of the agenda of the Conservatives. Part of the difficulty with such positions relates to the premises from which they start, which reveal some extraordinary misunderstandings of the nature of the post-war welfare settlement. The lack of historical perspective can be illustrated by the IPPR publication cited above (p. 142). The authors argue that in developing their proposals they have concentrated on ways to enhance people's life chances: 'as a result we emphasise the role of the State as a "trampoline", helping people and companies leap forward, and not its traditional role as a "safety net" for the market's social and economic victims' (Blackstone et al. 1992: 7). This suggests that welfare services were envisaged in the post-war settlement as residual services for the poor. Nothing could have been further from the truth: most clearly the NHS was designed as a universal service; equally, the Beveridge Report was a break from inter-war social-security schemes because it was universal in coverage; health and unemployment insurance and contributory pensions all operated with income limits in the inter-war period. The social services were a 'trampoline' and not a residual service, but then it was called universalism!

This failure to appreciate the intellectual basis of welfare services leads us to the first suggestion for a change of agenda. As was argued earlier, Labour has embraced consumerism, and this feature is included in the kinds of proposal embodied in the 1992 manifesto. It has already been argued that this is a false basis for the discussion of social services because it fails to grasp their social role. For example, in 1990 nearly 60 per cent of student entrants were drawn from social classes I and II, nearly 90 per cent of university students were under 21 (Smithers and Robinson 1991: Chart 6.6; UCCA 1990). This has an obvious individual dimension in the denial of opportunity to a wider range of groups in terms of class and age. It also has a social dimension in that it turns the university into a middle-class ghetto where a narrow range of social experience is reflected and a similarly narrow range of prejudices reinforced. This kind of example means that the questions which are asked about social welfare institutions should be vitally concerned with the social relations which they generate and the extent to which they reinforce genuine citizenship.

The second suggestion is related to another strange feature of the contemporary consensus. It has become increasingly fashionable to talk about 'empowerment': the *Citizen's Charter* and its Labour counterparts use such language. On the other hand, such terms are used in a context in which millions of our fellow citizens are condemned to unemployment. Table 6.1 illustrates the trend over the 1980s:

**Table 6.1** Unemployment in the United Kingdom, 1981–92

|          | Department of Employment count | Unemployment Unit count |
|----------|-------------------------------|-------------------------|
| May 1981 | 2,558,400 | n/a |
| May 1982 | 2,969,400 | n/a |
| May 1983 | 3,049,000 | 3,355,400 |
| May 1984 | 3.084,500 | 3,459,300 |
| May 1985 | 3,240,900 | 3,629,300 |
| May 1986 | 3,270,900 | 3,715,600 |
| May 1987 | 2,986,500 | 3,548,800 |
| May 1988 | 2,426,900 | 3,057,500 |
| May 1989 | 1,802,500 | 2,575,200 |
| May 1990 | 1,578,500 | 2,493,400 |
| May 1991 | 2,213,700 | 3,287,600 |
| May 1992 | 2,707,900 | 3,816,100 |

*Source*: Unemployment Bulletin, July 1992

The unemployment figures themselves are contentious because of the large number of definitional changes which were effected over the 1980s. To attempt to adjust for these changes the Unemployment Unit has constructed its own index, which is an estimate of what the unemployment level would be if these definitional changes had not occurred. It is clear from either count that mass unemployment has been a consistent feature of the 1980s. Even on the Department of Employment count unemployment did not fall below 1,5 million over the period. At the time of writing the United Kingdom is in recession for the second time in a just over a decade with obvious effects of unemployment.

Both Conservative and Labour Parties want to 'empower' citizens and yet both effectively accept mass unemployment as a given. A second element in a change of agenda is thus to re-establish the link between the economic and the social by putting the creation of employment at the top of the political agenda. In particular in this respect Labour policy is incoherent. If a deflationary agenda is accepted for the British and EC economy, it is difficult to see how key social objectives can be achieved. After all, unemployment is a formidable negative redistributive mechanism. In this respect one of the ultimate ironies of contemporary managerialism is provided by the 'Charter for Jobseekers', where staff are encouraged to wear 'corporate ties and scarves' when advising the unemployed. Vacancies may be a shade more difficult to arrange (Unemployment Unit 1991: 3).

An emphasis on employment creation will not work if old national forms are used. Thus, another paradox of the 'modernised' Labour Party is that, where it is distinctive from the Conservatives is in its emphasis on national policy instruments, like boosts to vocational training and domestic industrial investment (K. Williams et al. 1992; Cutler 1992b). However, mass unemployment is an EC-wide problem, which can only be resolved at that level. Equally, in an economy of unequal economic performance, sustained growth in employment will involve generating mechanisms which redistribute economic activity within the community and combat the powerful forces for centralisation of economic activity. (For a discussion of the position of Germany with respect to centralisation of economic activity in the EC, see Cutler et al. 1989: ch. 1).

The third point at which a change in agenda is needed is with respect to another premise of public sector consumerism. What is often argued is that the 'traditional' welfare state was concerned with meeting basic needs but that, with increasing affluence, this phase is effectively over, and what is now needed is a more 'customised' approach to welfare services, which learns from private sector service provision. However, again, it is worth investigating the underlying assumption here: Have basic needs been met?

One problem relates back to unemployment. It is surely difficult to argue that we are meeting basic needs when there is a mass unemployment problem. It is also relevant to consider the treatment of benefits. In the case of unemployment benefit, for example, a sharp fall in the real value of the benefit occurred in particular with the abolition of the

Earnings Related Supplement (ERS) in 1982. Thus, in April 1992 the unemployment benefit for a married couple (receiving average ERS prior to abolition) was only two-thirds of its November 1979 level (Unemployment Unit 1992: 14). Mass unemployment means that unemployment benefit is less significant with over 60 per cent of claimants in 1990 entirely dependent on income support (ibid.). In this respect there have been increases in benefit in real terms, but they have been modest when set against increases in earnings: in April 1992 the income support rate for a married couple with two children (aged 5 and 10) was 14.7 per cent higher than the corresponding supplementary benefit level in November 1979. However, over the same period average gross weekly earnings rose by 37.6 per cent. In November 1979 this supplementary benefit rate was 47 per cent of the average adult average wage; the corresponding figure for income support in 1992 was 34 per cent (Unemployment Unit 1992: 15). Equally, the 1990 Family Expenditure Survey showed that, on average, unemployed households were spending £20.42 per week in excess of their income (ibid.). Whatever the pros and cons of 'customisation', it can hardly be claimed that the welfare state does not need to tackle the issue of 'basic needs'.

Finally, there is the question of managerialism. As was argued earlier, managerialism operates in a relation of abstraction to the activity to be 'managed'. A change of agenda requires inverting this order of priorities. It also means abandoning the demonology of 'producer groups'. Forms of organisation and management should be viewed as needing to be adjusted to the activity involved. This means that good organisational and management research and good practice should stem from an understanding of health care, social work, teaching and higher educational research. This will also involve an engagement with professionals. In part, managerialism fails because it is founded on suspicion and reductionism with respect to professionals: as professionals are self-serving, management must continually be seeking ways of controlling them. The premise is dubious. Professionals are imperfect, but that they are motivated purely by economic interests is scarcely tenable. None of this is an argument against critically questioning current practice. On the contrary, the condition for such an examination is a break with the cut-and-dried outlook of managerialism.

# Bibliography

Akehurst, R., Hutton, J. and Dixon, R. (1991) *Review of Evidence of Higher Costs of Healthcare Provision in Inner London and a Consideration of Implications for Competitiveness*, York: Health Economics Consortium

Allen, D., Harley, M. and Makinson, G. (1987) 'Performance Indicators in the National Health Service', *Social Administration*, 21:1, pp. 70–84

Anonymous (1992) 'Gain Without Pain', *Health Service Journal*, 30 January, p. 25

Ascher, K. (1987) *The Politics of Privatisation: Contracting out Public Services*, London: Macmillan

Audit Commission (1983) *Performance Review in Local Government: a Handbook for Auditors and Local Authorities*, London: HMSO

_____ (1984) *Securing Further Improvements in Refuse Collection*, London: HMSO

_____ (1986) *Making a Reality of Community Care*, London: HMSO

_____ (1987) *Competitiveness and Contracting out of Local Authorities' Services*, London: HMSO

_____ (1988) *The Competitive Council*, London: HMSO

_____ (1992) Citizens' Charter: *Performance Indicators*, London: Audit Commission

Bach, S. (1989) *Too High a Price to Pay? A Study of Competitive Tendering for Domestic Services in the NHS*, Coventry: Industrial Relations Research Unit (University of Warwick)

Bacon, R. and Eltis, W. (1978) *Britain's Economic Problem*: *Too Few Producers*, Basingstoke: Macmillan

Bailey, R. and Trinder, C. (1989) *Under Attack? Public Sector Pay over Two Decades*, London: Public Finance Foundation

Bargaining Report (1990) *Compulsory Competitive Tendering – the effect on Wages and Conditions*, May, pp. 5–11

Barnett, R. (1988) 'Entry and Exit Performance Indicators for Higher

Education: some Policy and Research Issues', *Assessment and Evaluation in Higher Education*, 13:1, pp. 16–30

Basford, P. and Downie, C. (1991) 'How to Prepare a Business Plan', *Nursing Times*, 5 June, p. 63

Beardshaw, V. (1991) *The Impact of the NHS Reforms in London. Submission by the King's Fund to the House of Commons Select Committee on Health*, London: King's Fund

Beaumont, P.B. (1992) *Public Sector Industrial Relations*, London: Routledge

Becher, T. and Kogan, M. (1992) *Process and Structure in Higher Education* London: Routledge (2nd edition)

Birch, S. and Maynard, A. (1986) 'Performance Indicators in the UK National Health Service', *International Journal of Health Planning and Management* 1:2, pp. 143–56

Blackstone, T., Cornford, J., Hewitt, P. and Miliband, D. (1992) *Next Left: an Agenda for the 1990s*, London: Institute of Public Policy Research

Booth, T. (1990) 'Taking the Plunge', *Community Care*, 26 July, pp. 23–5

Bootle, R. (1981) 'How Important is it to Defeat Inflation? – the Evidence', *Three Banks Review* 132, pp. 23–47

Bosanquet, N. (1984) 'Social Policy and the Welfare State', in R. Jowell and C. Airey (eds), *British Social Attitudes: the 1984 Report*, London: Social and Community Planning Research

Bragg, C. (1988) 'Tendering Makes a Clean Sweep', *Health Services Journal*, 24 March, pp. 336–7

Brown, W. (1991) 'Industrial Relations', in M. Artis and D. Cobham (eds), *Labour's Economic Policy 1974–79*, Manchester: Manchester University Press

—— and Rowthorn, R. (1990) *A Public Services Pay Policy*, London: Fabian Society (Fabian Tract 542)

Burton, J. (1984) *Why No Cuts?*, London: Institute of Economic Affairs

Butler, D. (1989) *British General Elections Since 1945*, Oxford: Basil Blackwell

Caines, E. (1991) 'NHS Reforms: the Birth of Local Pay Determination', *Public Finance and Accountancy*, 26 July, pp. 14–17

Carter, N. (1989) 'Performance Indicators: 'Backseat Driving' or 'Hands Off Control', *Policy and Politics*, 17:2,pp. 131–138

—— (1991) 'Learning to Measure Performance: the Use of Indicators in Organisations', *Public Administration*, 69:1, pp. 85–103

Cave, M., Hanney, S. and Kogan, M. (1991) *The Use of Performance Indicators in Higher Education: a Critical Analysis of Developing*

*Practice*, London: Jessica Kingsley (2nd Edition)

Central Statistical Office (1991) 'Employment in the Public and Private Sectors', *Economic Trends*, 458, pp. 98–105

_____ (1992) *Social Trends,* 22, London: Government Statistical Service

Chandler, T. and Feuille, P. (1991) 'Municipal Unions and Privatization', *Public Administration Review*, 51:1, pp. 15–22

Chubb, J. and Moe, T. (1990) *Politics, Markets and America's Schools*, Washington, DC: Brookings Institution

Cole, I. and Welsh, D. (1991) 'Housing Indicators: Can They Perform?', *Public Finance and Accountancy*, 22 March, pp. 13–14

Committee of Vice Chancellors and Principals (1985) *Report of the Steering Committee for Efficiency Studies in Universities* (Jarratt Report), London: Committee of Vice Chancellors and Principals

Connelly, N. (1990) *Between Apathy and Outrage: Voluntary Organisations in Multiracial Britain*, London: Policy Studies Institute

Conservative Party (1992) *The Best Future for Britain*, London: Conservative Central Office

Conway, M. and Knox, C. (1990) 'Measuring Housing Effectiveness: a Case Study in Customer Evaluation', *Housing Studies*, 5:4, pp. 257–72

Courcouf, L. (1991) 'Tender Challenges', *Municipal Review and AMA News* June, pp. 59–62

Cubbin, J., Domberger, S. and Meadowcroft, S. (1987) 'Competitive Tendering and Refuse Collection: Identifying the Sources of Efficiency Gains', *Fiscal Studies*, 8:3, pp. 49–58

Cutler, T. (1992a) *Numbers in a Time of Dearth: Using Performance Indicators to 'Manage' Higher Education*, Paper presented at the 10th Annual Conference on the Organisation and Control of the Labour Process, University of Aston, April

_____ (1992b) 'Vocational Training and British Economic Performance: a Further Instalment of the "British Labour Problem"?', *Work, Employment and Society*, 6:2, pp. 161–83

_____, Haslam, C., Williams, J. and Williams, K. (1989) *1992– The Struggle for Europe: a Critical Evaluation of the European Community*, Oxford: Berg

_____, Williams, K. and Williams, J. (1986) *Keynes, Beveridge and Beyond*, London: Routledge and Kegan Paul

Department of Education and Science (1985) *The Development of Higher Education into the 1990s*, London: HMSO

_____ (1988) *Education Reform Act: Local Management of Schools*, Circular No. 7/88, London: Department of Education and Science

Department of Employment (1985) *Employment: the Challenge for the*

*Nation*, Cmnd. 9474, London: HMSO

Department of the Environment (1991) *Local Government Act 1988 Part 1. Competition in the Provision of Local Authority Services*, Circular 1/91, London: Department of the Environment

Department of Health (1989a) *Working for Patients*, CM. 555, London: HMSO

—— (1989b) *Funding and Contracts for Hospital Services*: Working Paper 2, London: HMSO

—— (1989c) *Practice Budgets for General Medical Practioners*: Working Paper 3, London: HMSO

—— (1989d) *Caring for People: Community Care in the Next Decade*, CM. 849, London: HMSO

—— (1990a) *Contracts for Health Services: Operating Contracts*, London: HMSO

—— (1990b) *Community Care in the Next Decade and Beyond: Practice Guidance*, London: HMSO

Department of Health and Social Services Inspectorate (1991a) *Purchase of Service: Practice Guidance*, London: HMSO

Department of Health/Price Waterhouse (1991b) *Implementing Community Care: Purchaser, Commissioner and Provider Roles*, London: HMSO

Department of Health (1992a) *Memorandum on the Financing of Community Care:Arrangements after April 1993 and on Individual Choice of Residential Accommodation*, London: Department of Health

Department of Health (1992b) *Report of the Inquiry into London's Health Service, Medical Education and Research*, London: HMSO

Department of Health and Social Security (1983) *Health Service Management: Competitive Tendering in the Provision of Domestic, Catering and Laundry Services*, HC (83) 18, London: DHSS

Dixon, R. (1991)'Repercussions of LMS', *Educational Management and Administration*, 19:1, pp. 52–61

Domberger, S., Meadowcroft, S. and Thompson, D. (1988) 'Competition and Efficiency in Refuse Collection: a Reply', *Fiscal Studies*, 9:2, pp. 86–90

Donahue, J. (1989) *The Privatization Decision*, New York: Basic Books

Eccleshall, R. (1990) *English Conservatism since the Restoration: an Introduction and Anthology*, London: Unwin-Hyman

Employment Department (1988) *Employment for the 1990s*, CM. 540, London: HMSO

Enthoven, A. (1978) 'Consumer Choice Health Care Plan', *New England Journal of Medicine*, 298: 12, pp. 650–8

_____ (1985) *Reflections on the Management of the National Health Service*, London: Nuffield Provincial Hospitals Trust

Erman, D. (1988) 'Hospital Utilization Review: Past Experience, Future Directions', *Journal of Health Politics, Policy and Law*, 13:4, pp. 683–704

Flynn, N. (1986)'Performance Measurement in Public Sector Services', *Policy and Politics*, 4:3, pp. 389–404

_____ (1990) *Public Sector Management*, London: Harvester-Wheatsheaf

_____ and Common, R. (1990) *Contracts for Community Care*, London: Department of Health

Foreman, D. (1991) 'Pricing up Performance', *Managing Schools Today*, 1:4, pp. 8–9

Fretwell, L.(1988) 'Contracting Out gets a Boost', *Local Government Chronicle*, 8 July (Supplement), pp. 3–33

Gallagher, A. (1991) 'Comparative Value Added as a Performance Indicator', *Higher Education Review*, 23:3, pp. 19–31

Ganley, J and Grahl, J. (1988) 'Competition and Efficiency in Refuse Collection: a Critical Comment', *Fiscal Studies*, 9:2 pp. 80–5

Green, D. (1988) *Everyone a Private Patient*, London: Institute of Economic Affairs

_____ (1990) 'A Missed Opportunity', in D. Green, J. Neuberger, M. Young and M. Burstall, *The NHS Reforms: Whatever Happened to Consumer Choice?*, London: Institute of Economic Affairs

Griffiths, R. (1983) *NHS Management Inquiry*, London: DHSS

Griffiths, R. (1988) Community Care: Agenda for Action, London: HMSO

Gutch, R. (1992) *Contracting Lessons from the US*, London: National Council for Voluntary Organisations

Ham, C. (1991) *The Impact of the NHS Reforms on Health Authorities and Trusts. Submission by the King's Fund to the House of Commons Select Committee on Health*, London: King's Fund

_____ (1992) 'Doctors' power, patients' risk', *The Guardian*, 25 March, p. 23

Harris, R. and Seldon, A. (1987) *Welfare Without the State: a Quarter of a Century of Suppressed Public Choice*, London: Institute of Economic Affairs

Harrison, S. (1988) *Managing the National Health Service; Shifting the Frontier*, London: Chapman and Hall

_____ and Wistow, G., (1992) 'The Purchaser/Provider Split in English Health Care: Towards Explicit Rationing?', *Policy and Politics*, 20:2, pp. 123–30

Hayek, F. (1960) *The Constitution of Liberty*, London: Routledge and

Kegan Paul

_____ (1967) *Studies in Philosophy, Politics and Economics*, London: Routledge and Kegan Paul

_____ (1976) *Law, Legislation and Liberty: a New Statement of the Liberal Principles of Justice and Political Economy* Volume 2. *The Mirage of Social Justice*, London: Routledge and Kegan Paul

_____ (1978) *New Studies in Philosophy, Politics, Economics and the History of Ideas*, London: Routledge and Kegan Paul

Health Committee (1991) *Public Expenditure on Health and Personal Social Services*, Third Report. Session 1990–91, HC 614–1, London HMSO

Hollingsworth, J. (1986) *A Political Economy of Medicine: Great Britain and the United States*, Baltimore: Johns Hopkins University Press

Hudson, B. (1992) 'Quasi-Markets in Health and Social Care in Britain: Can the Public Sector Respond?', *Policy and Politics*, 20:2, pp. 131–42

Income Data Services (1991) *Pay in the Public Sector*, London: Income Data Services

Interim Advisory Committee on School Teachers' Pay and Conditions (1988) *First Report*, CM. 363, London: HMSO

_____ (1990) *Third Report*, CM. 973, London: HMSO

_____ (1991) *Fourth Report*, CM. 1415, London: HMSO

Jarrett Report, see Committee of Vice Chancellors and Principals (1985)

Jenkins, L. , Bardsley, M. , Coles, J. and Wickings, I. (1988) *How Did We Do? The Use of Performance Indicators in the National Health Service*, London: CASPE Research

Jesson, D., Gray, J., Ranson, S. and Jones, B. (1985) 'Some Determinants of Variations in Expenditure on Secondary Education', *Policy and Politics*, 13:4, pp. 359–91

Johnson, L. (1991) *Contracts for Care: Issues for Black and other Ethnic Minority Groups*, London: National Council of Voluntary Organisations

Kerley, L. and Wynn, D. (1991) 'Competitive Tendering – the Transition to Contracting in Scottish Local Authorities', *Local Government Studies*, 17:5, pp. 33–51

Kessler, I. and Purcell, J. (1992) 'Performance Related Pay: Objectives and Application', *Human Resource Management Journal*, 2:3, pp. 16–33

King's Fund (1988) *Efficiency in the NHS: a Study of Cost Improvement Programmes*, London: King's Fund

_____ (1992) *London Health Care 2010*, London: King's Fund

Klein, R. (1982) 'Performance, Evaluation and the NHS: a Case Study in Conceptual Perplexity and Organizational Complexity', *Public Administration*, 60:4, pp. 385–407

Knapp, M. and Missiakoulis, S. (1982),'Inter-Sectoral Cost Comparisons: Day Care for the Elderly', *Journal of Social Policy*, 11:3. pp. 335–54

Labour Party (1987) *Britain Will Win*, London: The Labour Party

\_\_\_\_ (1992) *It's Time to Get Britain Working Again*, London: The Labour Party

Labour Research Department (1992a) 'Performance Related Pay', *Labour Research*, 81:3, p. 29

\_\_\_\_ (1992b) 'Who's in a Union?', *Labour Research*, 81:6, pp. 11–12

\_\_\_\_ (1992c) 'The Squeeze on Resources in Higher Education', *Labour Research*, 81:8, pp. 11–12

Laing, W. (1991) *Empowering the Elderly: Direct Consumer Funding of Care Services*, London: Institute of Economic Affairs

Lapsley, I. and Llewellyn, S. (1991) 'Accounting and Regulation in Local Government: the Case of Direct Labour Organisations', *Public Money and Management*, 11:4, pp. 43–52

\_\_\_\_ (1992) 'Government Policy and the Changing Market in Residential Care for the Elderly: a Financial Analysis of the Private Sector', *Financial Accountability and Management*, 8:2, pp. 97–113

Laver, M. (1984) 'On Party Polarisation and the Breaking of Moulds: the 1983 British Party Manifestos in Context', *Parliamentary Affairs*, 37, pp. 33–9

Le Grand, J. (1990) *Quasi-Markets and Social Policy*, Bristol: School of Advanced Urban Studies

Lewis, P. (1991) 'Performance Related Pay: Pretexts and Pitfalls', *Employee Relations*, 13:1, pp. 12–16

Local Authorities Conditions of Service Advisory Board (1990) *Performance Related Pay in Practice: Case Studies from Local Government*, PRP Report No. 3, London: LACSAB

Local Government Management Board (1992) *CCT Information Service Report No. 5*, London: Local Government Management Board

London Region Social Services Research Group (1989) 'Performance Indicators: Services for Children', *Research Policy and Planning*, 7:2, pp. 1–15

Macgregor, J. (1991) 'Spare Capacity', *Municipal Review and AMA News,* June, pp. 60–1

Marsh, D. (1991) 'Privatization under Mrs Thatcher: a Review of the Literature', *Public Administration*, 69:4, pp. 459–480

Mays, N. (1987) 'Measuring Needs in the National Health Service

Resource Allocation Formula: Standardised Mortality Ratios or Social Deprivation?', *Public Administration*, 65:1, pp. 45–60

McGuirk, T. (1991) 'Is the Private Sector Cleaning up on CCT?', *Public Finance and Accountancy*, 30 August, pp. 15–17

Mcpherson, A. (1992) *Measuring Added Value in Schools*, London: National Commission on Education, (NCE Briefing No. 1)

McSweeney, B. (1988) 'Accounting for the Audit Commission', *Political Quarterly*, 59:1, pp. 28–43

Meacher, M. (1992) *Diffusing Power: the Key to the Socialist Revival*, London: Pluto

Megaw (1982), see Report of an Inquiry into Civil Service Pay

Millar, B. (1991) 'Playing the Wild Card of Preferential Treatment', *Health Services Journal*, 30 May, p. 16

_____ (1992) 'A Price on Your Head', *Health Service Journal*, 9 July, p. 15

Miller, S. and Peroni, F. (1992) 'Social Politics and the Citizen's Charter', in N. Manning and R. Page (eds), *Social Policy Review 4*, Kent: Social Policy Association

Milne, R. (1987) 'Competitive Tendering in the NHS: an Economic Analysis of the Early Implementation of HC (83) 18, *Public Administration*, 65:2

Minogue, K. (1986) 'Politics and the Gross Intellectual Product', *Government and Opposition*, 21:4, pp. 396–405

Murlis, H. (1987) 'Performance Related Pay in the Public Sector', *Public Money*, 6:4, pp. 29–33

National Audit Office (1986) *Value for Money Developments in the NHS*, (HC 212), London: HMSO

_____ (1987) *Competitive Tendering for Support Services in the National Health Service* (HC 318), London: HMSO

_____ (1990) *The Elderly: Information Requirements for Supporting the Elderly and Implications for the National Insurance Fund of Personal Pensions* (HC 55), London: HMSO

Neale, A. (1992) 'Are British Workers Pricing Themselves out of Jobs?', *Work, Employment and Society*, 6:2, pp. 271–87

Nichols, T. (1986) *The British Worker Question*, London: Routledge and Kegan Paul

OECD (1987) *Historical Statistics 1960–1985*, Paris: OECD

O'Meara, R. (1992) *London's Legacy: Aspects of the NHS Estate in London*, London: King's Fund

Painter, J. (1991) 'Compulsory Competitive Tendering in Local Government: The First Round', *Public Administration*, 69:2, pp. 191–210

Parker, D. and Hartley, K. (1990) 'Competitive Tendering: Issues and Evidence', *Public Money and Management*, 10:3, pp. 9–14

Parkin, D. (1989) 'Comparing Health Efficiency across Countries', *Oxford Review of Economic Policy*, 5:1, pp. 75–88

Paton, C. (1992) *Competition and Planning in the National Health Service: The Danger of Unplanned Markets*, London: Chapman and Hall

*Pay and Benefits Bulletin* (1989) 'Performance-Related Pay Extends to NHS "Middle" Managers', 245, 5 December, p. 12

Phaure, S. (1991) *Who Really Cares?*, London: Voluntary Services Council

Phillimore, A. (1989) 'University Research Performance Indicators in Practice: The University Grants Committee's Evaluation of British Universities 1985–86', *Research Policy*, 18:5, pp. 255–71

Pollitt, C. (1986) 'Beyond the Managerial Model: The Case for Broadening Assessment in Government and Public Services', *Financial Accountability and Management*, 2:3, pp. 155–70

_____ (1990a) *Managerialism and the Public Services: The Anglo-American Experience*, Oxford: Basil Blackwell

_____ (1990b) 'Measuring University Performance: Never Mind the Quality: Never Mind the Width', *Higher Education Quarterly*, 44:1, pp. 60–81

_____ (1990c) 'Performance Indicators, Root and Branch', in M. Cave, M. Kogan and R. Smith (eds), *Output and Performance Measurement in Government: The State of the Art*, London: J. Kingsley

_____ Harrison, S., and Marmoch, P (1991) 'General Management in the NHS: The Initial Impact 1983–88', *Public Administration*, 69:1, pp. 61–85

Pratt, J. and Hillier, Y. (1991) *Bidding for Funds in the PCFC Sector*, London: Institute of Education

Priestley Commission, see Royal Commission on the Civil Service (1955)

Prime Minister's Office (1991) *The Citizen's Charter: Raising the Standard*, CM. 1599, London: HMSO

*Public Service Action* (1991) 'Business as Usual', February, p. 44

Qaiyoom, R. (1992) 'Contracting: a Black Perspective', *Contracting in or out?*, Spring, p. 5

Quam, L. (1989) 'Post-War American Health Care: The Many Costs of Market Failure', *Oxford Review of Economic Policy*, 5:1, pp. 113–23

Railings, C. and Thrasher, M. (1990) 'Contract Patterns', *Local Government Chronicle* (Supplement), 6 July, pp. 12–15

Report of an Inquiry into Civil Service Pay (1982) Volume 1, CŃD. 8590, London: HMSO (Megaw Report)

Review Body for Nursing Staff, Midwives and Health Visitors (1984) *First Report*, CND. 9258, London: HMSO

_____ (1985) *Second Report*, CND. 9529, London: HMSO

_____ (1987) *Fourth Report*, CM. 129, London: HMSO

_____ (1988) *Fifth Report*, CM. 360, London: HMSO

_____ (1989) *Sixth Report*, CM. 577, London: HMSO

_____ (1990) *Seventh Report*, CM. 934, London: HMSO

_____ (1991) *Eighth Report*, CM. 1411, London: HMSO

_____ (1992) *Ninth Report*, CM. 1811, London: HMSO

Review Body on Doctors' and Dentists' Renumeration (1983) *Thirteenth Report*, CND. 8878, London: HMSO

_____ (1984) *Fourteenth Report*, CND. 9256, London: HMSO

_____ (1987) *Seventeenth Report*, CM. 127, London: HMSO

_____ (1991) *Twenty First Report*, CM. 1412, London: HMSO

_____ (1992) *Twenty-Second Report*, CM. 1813, London: HMSO

Roberts, H. (1990) *Outcome and Performance in Health Care*, London: Public Finance Foundation

Robinson, R. (1990) *Competition and Health Care: A Comparative Analysis of UK Plans and US Experience*, London: King's Fund

Royal Commission on the Civil Service 1953–55 (1955), Cmd 9613, London: HMSO (Priestley Commission)

Saran, R. and Sheldrake, J. (eds) (1988) *Public Sector Bargaining in the 1980s*, Avebury: Gower

Scheuer, M. and Robinson, R. (1991) 'A Wild Card in the Pack?', *Health Services Journal*, 8 August, pp. 18–20

School Teachers' Review Body (1992) *First Report*, Cm. 1806, London: HMSO

Sherman, J. (1985) 'Waiting for the Big Bite', *Health and Social Service Journal*, 27 June, pp. 806–7

Simborg, D. (1981) 'DRG Creep: A New Hospital-Acquired Disease', *New England Journal of Medicine*, 304:15, pp. 1602–4

Smithers, A. and Robinson, P. (1991) *Beyond Compulsory Schooling: A Numerical Picture*, London: Council for Industry and Higher Education

Social Services Committee (1989) *Resourcing the National Health Service: The Government's Plans for the Future of the NHS*, Eighth Report, Session 1988/9, HC 214-11, London: HMSO

Social Services Committee (1990) *Community Care: Choice for Service Users*, Sixth Report, Session 1989/90, HC 444, London: HMSO

Stevens, B. (1978) 'Scale, Market Structure and the Cost of Refuse

Collection', *Review of Economics and Statistics*, LX:3, pp. 438–48

_____ (1984) 'Comparing Public and Private Sector Productive Efficiency: An Analysis of Eight Activities', *National Productivity Review*, 3:3, pp. 395–406

Taylor-Gooby, P. (1991) 'Attachment to the Welfare State', in R. Jowell, L. Brook, B. Taylor, with P. Prior (eds), *British Social Attitudes: The Eighth Report*, London: Social and Community Planning Research

Therborn, G. (1986) *Why Some Peoples Are More Unemployed Than Others*, London: Verso

Thirlwall, A. (1981) 'Keynesian Employment Theory is not Defunct', *Three Banks Review*, 132, pp. 14–29

Thomson, A.W.J. and Beaumont, P.B. (1978) *Public Sector Bargaining; a Study of Relative Gain*, Farnborough: Saxon House

Titmuss, R. (1968) *Commitment to Welfare*, London: George Allen and Unwin

Tomlinson, J. (1990) *Hayek and the Market*, London: Pluto

Treasury (1979) *Government Expenditure Plans* 1980–81 CMND. 1746, London: HMSO

_____ (1986) *Using Private Enterprise in Government: Report of a Multi-Departmental Review of Competitive Tendering and Contracting for Services in Government Departments*, London: HMSO

_____ (1991) *Competing for Quality Buying Better Public Services*, CM. 1730, London: HMSO

_____ (1992a) *The Governments Expenditure Plans 1992–93 to 1994–95: Departmental Report, Department of Education and Science*, CM. 1911, London: HMSO

_____ (1992b) *The Government's Expenditure Plans 1992–93 to 1994–95, Departmental Report, Department of Health*, CM. 1913, London: HMSO

UCCA (1990) *27th. Report 1985–89*, London: UCCA.

Unemployment Unit (1991) 'The Citizen's Charter and the Unemployed', *Working Brief*, 28, p. 3

_____ (1992) 'Real Value of Unemployment Benefits', *Working Brief*, 37, pp. 14–15

University Funding Council (1989) *Report on the 1989 Research Assessment Exercise*, London: University Funding Council

Waine, B. (1991) *The Rhetoric of Independence: The Ideology and Practice of Social Policy in Thatcher's Britain*, Oxford: Berg

Walsh, K. (1989) 'Competition and Service in Local Government', in J. Stewart and P. Stoker (eds), *The Future of Local Government*, London: Macmillan

Webb, S. (1901) 'Lord Roseberry's Escape From Houndsditch', *The Nineteenth Century and After*, 50, pp. 366–86

Wedderburn, W. (1986) *The Worker and the Law* (3rd edition), Harmondsworth: Penguin

_____ (1989) 'Freedom of Association and Philosophies of Labour Law', *Industrial Law Journal*, 18:1, pp. 1–38

Weiner, J.P. and Ferriss, D.M. (1990) *G.P. Budget Holding in the UK: Lessons from America*, London: King's Fund

Weiner, S. L., Maxwell, J. H., Sapolsky, H. M., Dunn, D. L. and Hsiao, W. C. (1987) 'Economic Incentives and Organisational Realities: Managing Hospitals Under DRGs', *The Milbank Quarterly*, 65:4, pp. 463–87

Wells, J. (1989) 'Official Statistics Indicate An Unprecedented Squeeze On NHS Resources Since 1981', *Financial Times*, 11 February

Williams, B. (1991) *University Responses To Research Selectivity*, London: Institute of Education

Williams, K. and Williams, J. (1987) 'M-Way Crash', *Times Higher Education Supplement*, 16 October

Williams, K., Williams, J., Cutler, T.and Haslam, C. (1992) *From National Autarky To European Integration? Labour's Policies in the 1980s and 1990s*, Paper presented at the Conference on 'Labour: The Party or Industrial Modernisation', London School of Economics, April

Wistow, G., Knapp, M., Hardy, B. and Allen, C. (1992) 'From Providing to Enabling: Local Authorities and the Mixed Economy of Social Care', *Public Administration*, 70:1, pp. 25–45

# INDEX